ETHICAL
TRIBING

Connecting the Next Generation
to Israel in the Digital Era

JOANNA LANDAU AND MICHAEL GOLDEN

Published by Best Seller Publishing®, St. Augustine, FL
Best Seller Publishing® is a registered trademark.
Printed in the United States of America.

ISBN: 978-1-959840-34-3

This publication is designed to provide accurate and authoritative information with regard to the subject matter covered. It is sold with the understanding that the publisher is not engaged in rendering legal, accounting, or other professional advice. If legal advice or other expert assistance is required, the services of a competent professional should be sought. The opinions expressed by the authors in this book are not endorsed by Best Seller Publishing® and are the sole responsibility of the authors rendering the opinion.

For more information, please write:
Best Seller Publishing®
53 Marine Street
St. Augustine, FL 32084
or call 1 (626) 765-9750
Visit us online at: www.BestSellerPublishing.org

This book is dedicated to the courageous visionaries who took bold action to establish and advance the modern State of Israel — and to the Jewish leaders of today who, in the face of growing adversity, will take the next great leap in order to safeguard the future of the Jewish People.

Contents

Foreword(s)

In this book, we talk a lot about how science and data can help us to communicate with the Next Generation. At the same time, we are always guided and inspired by *their own thoughts*. You will see their words and posts throughout *Ethical Tribing*, and it is in that spirit that we wanted you to hear directly from them on the very first page.

"Honestly, I don't think about Israel much at all but you hear all this bad stuff about it from people. But then, when I see videos on TikTok about what it's like there, it looks like a really cool place."

— Evelyn Gonzalez, 16, high school student,
Pittsburgh, Pennsylvania

"I would show the side of Israel that's more like the everyday life of a young person. Young kids don't want to be lectured. And you're not going to get a non-Jewish 22-year-old person to go to Israel because of the Western Wall. You'll get them to go there because of that incredibly unique experience I had when they turned the Shuk into a nightclub in like a minute! Show a different way of socializing. Fun stuff like that. That's the kind of stuff that we should advertise on social media."

— Ben Goldberg, 22, Chicago, Illinois

"Food tastes so much better when shared with friends. I will be forever grateful to (@vibeisrael for bringing me to Tel Aviv and introducing me to so many different cultures, delicious food with roots from all around the world but also because I had the opportunity to learn more about the Israeli people. Thank you for opening my horizon more and gifting me so many new friendships."

— Instagram post by Shabnam Reno, @thehungrywarrier, Persian-German vegan influencer who visited Israel in 2020

"I think anyone reading this will be familiar with at least the fact that there is a conflict in Israel. But did you know Israel is first in the world in water recycling? That there are more startups, cafes, museums, vegans, clean energy innovators, PHD holders, and theater tickets sold per capita than in any other country in the world? That it is host to the world's largest regional Burn? That it holds the Middle East's largest — and essentially only — gay pride events? The Israel I found was home to some of the most vibrant cities, stunning landscapes, and interesting people I've encountered on my travels. It was teeming with creative energy, filled with delicious healthy food, and bursting with a passion for the outdoors and adrenaline-pumping adventure activities."

"You just keep opening my eyes, gal, to the world out there! I'm really loving the way you describe the places, scenery, everything! I have never been to Israel, never thought about going but your post was very interesting to me! Ya got me wondering!"

— Excerpt and reply from a blog post by Alexandra Baackes, travel influencer who visited Israel in 2018

Authors' Note

It is important for us to note, right at the outset, that this book is not about Israel as it is reflected in its elections or geo-political policies. We hope that as you read it, you will take a step back and contemplate our suggestions from a long-range perspective. After all, the current Israeli government will not govern forever, nor will the ones that succeed it. Political currents change, new parties get formed, and officeholders get replaced — on both sides.

Israel is a Jewish and democratic state, and Ethical Tribing is a strategy that will outlive any particular government or political moment in time. So long as Israel remains a thriving democracy, the ideas presented in this book will apply.

Preface

This book is personal. There are no two ways about it.

In fact, the two of us would never have met in the first place had it not been so personal. We lead different family lives, with different careers, on different continents, under different political systems.

What we share is the very deepest concern that the future of the Jewish People and the State of Israel are under a new and urgent threat: for several years now, we have been witnessing sagging levels of both Jewish identity and connection to Israel amongst the Next Generation. These two phenomena have been growing steadily, side by side. Taken together, they form no less than an existential danger to our Tribe.

The nature of this growing drift makes the mission for our community very clear: start reversing these troubling trends right now, before they become irreversible. The clock is ticking.

The hopeful news is that an achievable solution exists to meet this challenge. We call it "Ethical Tribing," and it is the fastest and most effective way to connect the Next Generation (people aged forty and under) to Israel in the digital era.

It is a strategy based on the science of influence that harnesses the power of social media to tell Israel's story in a way that creates new levels of appeal and appreciation for it — not least amongst those who will carry forward the mantle of Jewish Peoplehood for decades to come.

The essential benefit of cultivating this new and renewed affection for Israel is the expansion of people's capacity to accept it in its entirety — to view and treat Israel with the same levels of respect and fairness that are extended to so many other sovereign states in the community of nations.

Throughout this book, we are going to take you through the Ethical Tribing strategy, step-by-step. But first, precisely because this mission is so very personal, we would like to tell you a little bit more about ourselves and how two different backgrounds so easily meshed behind one common vision.

JOANNA'S STORY: CHOOSING ISRAEL

"Of all the countries in the world, why do you choose to live in Israel?" he asked.

It was a reasonable question to ask a British-born Israeli, with roots strongly embedded in the United Kingdom.

My great-grandfather had built himself up out of poverty to become a successful businessman, and my grandfather took over from him and turned the business global. My grandmother was deeply involved in local politics. My parents, who had met in London, decided to move to Israel when I was very young, around five years old. It was their decision, not mine. They scooped up my brother and me and settled in Ramat Hasharon, a suburb north of Tel Aviv.

I grew up in a lovely neighborhood in the 1980s in Israel — a provincial country back then, with maybe two or three really good restaurants, long before it earned the moniker *Start-Up Nation*. But I felt too English in Israel. People would bump into me on the street, and my British reaction was of course to apologize, which caused the average Israeli *sabra* (born in Israel) to look at me with dismay. Every time we would go back to London to visit my grandparents, I would feel the difference between the energy and global standard of this more dynamic, advanced city and that sleepy suburb I lived in.

I had a wonderful childhood. It was effortless and informal, but that feeling of not fitting in led me to choose to finish my high school years at a Jewish boarding school in Oxfordshire, England. It was when I returned to Israel to complete my compulsory military service in the Israel Defense Forces that living in Israel finally became *my* choice.

That experience in the IDF made me feel a part of something; I was now a strong, confident Jew living in my own country. That, compared with the Jew-as-a-minority experience of living in the UK, was what first connected me to Israel. But that's not the only reason I choose to live here.

After the army, I earned bachelor's and master's degrees in law from Cambridge University. When I returned to Israel, I interned at a leading law firm that represented start-ups. Being a part of the growing tech bubble was a thrilling experience;

the energy was palpable. And it was during this time that Israel became more cosmopolitan, improved its standards to welcome international businesspeople, and began to catch up with more developed countries.

I had met my American-born Israeli husband after my first year at university, and we got married within a year of my return to Israel, when I was twenty-five. By the time I was thirty-three, we had three children and were living in Tel Aviv. As we were raising our kids, I earned an MBA at Reichman University and launched a couple of start-ups, and I was keeping myself busy.

But something was missing.

When I was thirty-five years old, I woke up one morning and said to myself:

> "I'm a passionate person, but I don't know what I'm passionate about."

That led me on a journey of self-discovery to find out what my real calling was — what I truly wanted to do with my life. I had a few meetings with a life coach, and that was the first time I was asked that question:

> "Of all the countries in the world, why choose Israel?"

I didn't really know how to articulate my answer back then. But now I do. And the reason I do is that Michael Golden, my co-author in this effort, asked me that very same question, just over a decade later.

In the dozen years since I was first challenged with that question, I have dedicated my life to connecting young people to

Israel using positive, inspiring messaging and digital strategies through the nonprofit I established: Vibe Israel. I continue to be fully committed to this mission through my work with Israel's stakeholders and anyone who is involved in positively promoting Israel on a global scale. It was through that work that I came to learn why I chose — and continue to choose — Israel.

I choose Israel because I love the energy of this country. I love that when I'm in a taxicab, at the top of the hour, the driver will turn up the radio volume so we can both listen to the news. That may not seem like a good thing to many, because it means you're waiting to hear if there's anything to be concerned about. But it also means that you and this person that you don't know — both of you *care*. We're somehow connected to this place, so much so that we want to know what's going on with it at any given time.

I choose Israel because I don't need to actively practice my Judaism and yet I'm very Jewish here, in the non-religious, more cultural sense. Though we light candles, and bless the wine and bread on Friday nights, I don't necessarily relate to the words we read, even though I understand what they mean because they're in the language my forefathers have spoken for thousands of years. We don't keep Shabbat, and I am not kosher. I can be totally secular in Israel and still not have to look up the exact dates of Jewish holy days such as Hanukkah or Yom Kippur because they just form a part of my life. It's easier being Jewish in Israel.

I choose Israel because my eyes well up with tears of joy and my heart bursts with national pride when I take part in Independence Day celebrations. But it also beats with tremendous sadness twenty-four hours earlier, on Memorial Day for the Fallen Soldiers and Victims of Hostile Acts, expressing a collective sorrow that means I'm a part of something bigger than myself. I love that Memorial Day isn't about shopping or materialism, but is genuinely about remembering the sacrifice of others.

I choose Israel because of the vibrancy of Tel Aviv, the calming stillness of the Negev desert, the leafy beauty of the Galilee and Golan Heights — all places that I can visit without flying or driving for six hours. It's a small country, but one that envelops my family and makes us feel bigger.

I choose Israel for the amazing culinary scene, the vibrant culture, and the unrelenting entrepreneurial zeal of the Israelis. We are a people who punch above our weight to the point of exhaustion.

And even during those times when it's really tough and it feels like I might want to give up, there's always someone or something that reminds me why I make this choice, every single day.

Ultimately, it is the pride I feel in being Jewish that drives my choice: to live in a country that was built by and for the Jewish People, and is a vibrant democracy that recognizes — not without fault — its responsibility to observe the rights of everyone who lives here.

As long as Israel remains a Jewish and democratic country, I will choose to live here.

———————————

The path that led me to the more recent contemplation of the "choose Israel" question was paved a year earlier when a trusted Vibe board member in America, Alicia Oberman, insisted on introducing me to Michael. She told me that he was not only an award-winning journalist and political strategist, but also a fellow Jew who cared deeply about the future of Israel and the Jewish people. Alicia put us on the phone, and in under five minutes, Michael fully grasped the Vibe strategy. He has been a valued partner to us ever since.

I asked Michael to co-write this book not only because of his long experience in harnessing strategic communications to build mission-driven organizations — but also because of the fresh, Jewish American perspective he brings to the subject. What I bring to our effort is more than a decade's experience engaging the Next Generation with Israel (primarily on digital platforms), professional expertise in the realm of country and city branding, and a can-do, Israeli approach.

Israel is a young, exciting country, yet the conversations about it that happen outside of its borders are usually framed through the very narrow lens of religion and politics. Why is this the case? Why does the spotlight always seem to shine on Israel's shortcomings, rather than on its strengths? Why is it that most people *do not* choose Israel? And perhaps more dramatically, why are some members of the Jewish Next Gen not choosing Israel, like most of their parents and grandparents did?

In this book, we take a good look in the mirror to answer these questions — and then we present a detailed strategy that is designed to turn the tables.

The fact is that at times our community has a tendency to blame anti-Semitism, the media coverage, or the Boycott, Divestment, Sanctions (BDS) movement, for this state of affairs. While we know that each of these play substantial roles in people's perceptions of Israel, I find focusing on them alone to be incredibly limiting. For, if it's always someone else's doing, it will always be too easy to lose hope because we've conceded that it's out of our control. But if we look at this problem as something that is within our ability to change, we can proactively decide that it is *our* responsibility to do so. And it is that decision that opens up a world of opportunity to shape our people's future.

Today, I truly believe that we — the Jewish People in the Diaspora, the State of Israel and the Israeli people — are not doing enough to get the message out there. To give young Jews and non-Jews a good enough reason to *want* to see Israel positively. To actively choose Israel. **It's up to us to claim our positive space in global attention and perception.**

If we won't do it, why should we expect anyone else to?

I believe the downward trend in perceptions of Israel, among young people the world over (especially amongst Next Gen Jews in North America) can be inverted. But to do this, we must recognize that what's needed is nothing less than a bold paradigm shift in the way that we view the entire challenge. And we need a strategy. A strong, tried-and-tested strategy to implement assertively and with the collective belief that it will deliver.

There's a sentence that I take with me everywhere I go since I embarked on my journey. It was said by Victor Hugo, the French philosopher and playwright:

"All the forces in the world are not so powerful as an idea whose time has come."

Michael and I believe that the Ethical Tribing strategy is *an idea whose time has come*. And we hope that by the time you finish this book, you, too, will feel confident about this strategy's potential to inspire the Next Gen — especially those within our Tribe — to choose Israel, quickly and effectively.

It's a wonderful feeling to know, in your heart of hearts, that change is possible. But as they say, it takes a village.

Together, we can make it go viral.

MICHAEL'S STORY: OUR HOME IS OUR FUTURE

It was an icy night in Chicago more than twenty-five years ago when I first interviewed a survivor of the Holocaust. Margot and Charles Schlesinger were two out of the 1,200 *Schindler-Juden* who had survived the Shoah under the protection of industrialist Oskar Schindler.

As the three of us talked about Steven Spielberg's new film, *Schindler's List*, Mrs. Schlesinger described the scene that for her was the most chillingly real to watch:

"Auschwitz was the most moving part, because I was there. And I didn't know whether there was water or gas coming out of the pipes. And it was horrifying to see the kids being taken to Auschwitz to be gassed as the German lullaby was being played over the loudspeaker."

I will never forget Margot and Charles Schlesinger's words from that night, just as I will never forget the stories of the many Holocaust survivors whom I came to know and be awed by over the next three decades.

Just a few years later, in 1999, I found myself standing in Independence Hall in Tel Aviv, singing *Hatikva*. It was my first visit to Israel, which had just celebrated its 51st anniversary as the official State of the Jewish people. As I listened to the sound of Israel's national anthem, I could feel a knot swelling up in my throat. This was not my home country, yet the sense of national pride I felt at that moment was palpable.

Of the nearly 8 billion people on Earth today, just over 15 million are Jews. Each of us has our own story and personal connection to Judaism. And we all have our own definition of what it means to be Jewish.

In my case, I was born in 1967 at Chicago's Mount Sinai Hospital to two Jewish parents. I grew up as a Reform Jew, the most liberal strand of Judaism. My family celebrated a handful of Jewish holidays and I attended Hebrew school through age thirteen, when I became a bar mitzvah. Yet, as with so many Jewish Americans over the past few decades, those early years of Reform practice did not inspire in me a deep sense of Jewish identity.

Ironically, it was a course on Jewish history during my time as an undergraduate that finally piqued my interest in what it meant to be a descendant of the Jewish people. Once I delved deeper into the backstory of how Jews had miraculously survived and rebuilt their Tribes again and again — from exile in Babylon to persecution under the Romans to the Spanish

Inquisition to Hitler's genocidal *Final Solution* — that's when my identity as a Jew really began to take root.

Of course, Jews fall across a wide spectrum when it comes to how and why we identify as Jewish. This is especially the case in America.[1] But the common tie that always seems to bind us is the shared sense of pride we take in our unlikely survival. Jewish existence is about far more than a formal religion; we are the *Jewish People*. By battling our way through an unremitting progression of existential threats and excruciating struggles — as well as by achieving exhilarating triumphs — the Jewish People have developed a uniquely rich culture and impregnable sense of community.

That seminal day when I met Margot and Charles Schlesinger set me on a course of caring about and becoming engaged in Jewish advocacy, mostly through "lay leadership." Over the years, I raised funds for the US Holocaust Memorial Museum, supported IDF soldiers, advised Jewish leaders on messaging and communications, and helped more survivors to share their experiences and wisdom with the world.

But the most eye-opening time that I spent in Jewish advocacy was when I worked full time in 2001–2002 as a public voice for the Anti-Defamation League's Midwest office. Across six states, the incoming assaults we pushed back against every day ran the gamut: attacks on Jewish elected officeholders, anti-Semitism on college campuses, the KKK's heinous marches, and so on. We were busy.

Unfortunately, and unsurprisingly, Jewish advocacy professionals are still busy. They are always busy. And I believe that the rest of us are in their debt. The work that they do is truly difficult — and unfailingly necessary. In fact, the incidence of anti-Semitic acts in the United States rose to a record high in 2021.[2]

We know how important traditional advocacy is in fighting anti-Semitism and in providing critical support to the State of Israel. But this is not one and the same with shaping how people *feel* about our home country as a whole. Especially young people. I'm not talking about changing the set opinions that many folks have about government policy. I'm talking about sharing with them everything else there is to love about Israel. While there is much daylight between these two missions, they are crucially related. One effort augments the other.

Many Jewish Americans have a very different sensibility than do Israeli Jews when it comes to beliefs about the best courses of action to defend and protect Israel. How could they not be different? There is no way for Americans to understand the complexities of living as a citizen of Israel — unless and until they've become a citizen of Israel.

Yet what we do share is **the imperative priority to always keep Israel as the indispensable home of the Jewish People**. Though the painful history that Jews have endured and survived shall never fully define us, there is no question that our people have learned how to convert the past into a constantly renewable source of energy to drive us forward.

It was during an impassioned conversation I was having about all of this with my friend Alicia that I met Joanna. As our exchange became more and more intense — we were in violent agreement — all of a sudden Alicia's face lit up and she started telling me about Vibe Israel and Joanna's vision for Israel. Then she called Joanna in the middle of the night in Tel Aviv and put me on the line. In minutes, a partnership was born.

After having worked as a television news reporter and political strategist for nearly twenty years, I have leveraged the power of storytelling again and again to deliver information — and to shape perspectives and decision-making. Understanding where an audience is coming from and then meeting them where they're at — so that a message will land and stick — is both a science and an art. Joanna and I clicked on this shared experience instantaneously.

Over the next year, as I worked with Joanna and her exceptional team, the value of her philosophy became even clearer to me. A bona fide visionary, she was at an inflection point where she was ready to take the decade-plus expertise she'd accrued as founder and CEO of Vibe Israel, and scale its reach and impact to a whole new level. Better yet, she'd already began assembling the elements of the formula.

When Joanna started mapping out the plan to put this mission on steroids to meet the urgency of the moment, that's when we became inspired to co-present this strategy we call Ethical Tribing. For without its adoption and expeditious application, we fear the Jewish People may be missing out on an irreplaceable opportunity to change not only the way that Israel is perceived — but how it is treated by other nations as a result.

It is a precarious time, as the Next Generation may be our final firewall. Yet we have a strategy to get there: a course we can chart to win millions of minds and hearts. All that we need is the will to cast off together and a commitment to keep steering the ship in the right direction.

On that first trip I took to Israel twenty years ago, I broke away from my travel mates one day to return to Yad Vashem. It was a sunny afternoon, and after exiting the museum, I sat down in an area known as Warsaw Ghetto Square. I gazed up at two visually breathtaking memorial sculptures titled *The Warsaw Ghetto Uprising* and *The Last March*. As I prayed for all of the souls that were stolen and the families that they were lost to, I scrawled down the following:

> "Even as I examined the enlarged, graphic photos in the museum exhibits, the concept of six million Jews being systematically annihilated is still difficult for my mind to grasp. 'Six million.' I've heard the number so many times and heard so many survivors tell me their stories — and yet it is still hard for me to process. I am so proud to have known these survivors, and I am proud to be a Jew. I have felt this pride every minute of every day since I arrived in Israel."

Twenty years later, that same sense of pride is what inspired me to take on this critically important project with Joanna. From the deepest part of our hearts, we believe in the potential that Ethical Tribing can deliver to the country that we love. And now, it is our job to make you believe.

For your open minds and your careful consideration of the case we are about to present, we most sincerely thank you.

Introduction

"The secret of change is to focus all of your energy not on fighting the old, but on building the new."

— Socrates

In 1956, when Cecil B. DeMille directed *The Ten Commandments*, he shattered the record for most expensive Hollywood film budget. As often happens with historical dramas, DeMille had to make decisions about what to include from the historical record — and what to change. And because of the way he portrayed the film's climactic scene, there are millions of people whose impression of the story of Exodus includes God parting the sea just seconds before the Hebrews were able to make safe passage across it.

DeMille probably made the right call. The film set records at the box office and has stood the test of time. But in doing so, he deprived a vast audience from experiencing one of the seminally inspiring stories of the Jewish People.

In the Talmudic account of those events, we learn that as the Hebrews were pinned down between the massive Egyptian Army and the Sea of Reeds, God commanded Moses to lead the Twelve Tribes of Israel straight into the waters.[1] But they hesitated; none wanted to be the first to risk their life. It wasn't until a man named Nachshon ben Aminadav jumped into the waves — and then became submerged above his nose — that God ordered Moses to lift his staff and spread his hand over the sea. Only at that point did the water divide, allowing the Israelites to cross unscathed, escaping Pharaoh's forces.

The name Nachshon derives from *nachshol*, the Hebrew word for "tidal wave." Facing the sea's peril, the son of Jacob did not hesitate; he bravely took action.

A little over three millennia later, in April 1948, a military mission known as "Operation Nachshon" was given the green light by the man who would become Israel's first prime minister, David Ben Gurion. Anticipating an attack on Jerusalem by Arab forces — they had already hamstrung the Jews' supply route from Tel Aviv — the Jewish paramilitary unit known as the Haganah prepared to execute its first major operation. Up against it, and with no time to dither, just like their operation's namesake, they did not hesitate. The brigade of 1,500 men conquered three Arab camps that were blockading the mountain road — and enabled the Jews to move critical supplies to the heart of Israel.

Again and again, the Jewish People have been forced to anticipate, innovate, and take bold action in order to survive. And thrive. Our Tribe has accomplished this by repeatedly adapting to the next challenge — at times unsure of our own path forward, yet never daunted.

As we send this blueprint out into the world, Israel is just months away from celebrating its 75th anniversary as the modern state of the Jewish People. The birth and astonishingly swift evolution of the State of Israel represent nothing short of a modern miracle driven by a relentlessly resilient people. Yet the promise of a long and prosperous future for any country — no matter how sinewy its citizenry — is the furthest thing from a guarantee. Jews, perhaps better than any other people on the planet, are well acquainted with this historical fact.

Jews in the United States and around the world have flourished over the past century. We've rightly celebrated these successes, yet they are never to be taken for granted. Anti-Semitism remains an ever-present threat. And it is rising rapidly.

According to the Anti-Defamation League,[2] in 2021 the United States saw an all-time high of anti-Semitic incidents: 2,717. Acts of assault, vandalism, and harassment were committed in all fifty states — and represented a 34 percent increase over 2020. Of the total, 525 incidents took place at Jewish institutions — a 61 percent increase over the year prior.

Jews who actively support Israel recognize this global trend as a stark reminder of how crucial it is for us to have *our own state* — with the authority and capability to ensure its security. Throughout history, even as we were making important contributions to the building of communities all over the world, Jews were nevertheless evicted from countless countries. For no other reason than for being Jewish.

Now, in the 21st century, having built a historic nation that is strong in so many ways — yet also faces new threats in a modern world — the Jewish community must innovate once again. We must take a deep look downfield and ask the hard questions: will our descendants be connected enough to their Jewish identity — and to Israel — to take the necessary steps to promote it and defend it? Will they have the strength in numbers and the wherewithal to protect the one country that stands tall as the common refuge for all Jews?

In this book, we will grapple with these questions and make clear the need for a solution. We will explain how members of the "Next Generation" are already gaining enormous power and influence over how the world perceives Israel — and how Israel is treated as a result.

Most of us over the age of fifty will have very limited direct impact over what happens to Israel in the second half of this century. On extolling its virtues. On inspiring new visitors to experience its culture and majesty. The Next Gen, however, will have that opportunity to shape how Israel is viewed — **if they care enough to get in the game.**

To be clear, there are many young people who care about their Jewish identity and about Israel — and we will need their help in this movement to appeal to the growing proportion who do not. The onus is on all of us to transport the great number of Next Gen'ers who feel *indifferent* toward Israel — both Jews and non-Jews — to the place where they feel a genuine affinity for it.

This objective can be accomplished through a strategy we call "Ethical Tribing." Working together, and using modern communication techniques, we can change the way that the world sees Israel.

Achieving this goal will lead to two correlated outcomes: strengthening Israel's status as a nation — and securing the future of the Jewish People.

THE LANDSCAPE

We define the Next Generation or "Next Gen" as people ranging in age from their late teens to forty. This demographic[3] basically encompasses the bulk of millennials (born after 1981) and those who make up Generation Z (born after 1997). All together in America, they number more than 110 million,[4] making up 33 percent of the US population. These will be the digital voices who shape media narratives about Israel and, by extension, public opinion for many decades to come. It is already happening.

Within that overall group, there are approximately 2.85 million Next Gen Jews, representing 38 percent of the total number of Jewish Americans: 7.5 million.[5] While the population figures for younger Jews have more or less held level over the past decade, there are troubling signs that among the Next Generation Jews in the Diaspora — especially in North America — the depth of Jewish identity and connection to Israel has been diminishing in recent decades.

A Pew Research Center survey from 2020 revealed that when eighteen- to twenty-nine-year-olds were asked how much being Jewish mattered to them, 67 percent answered "very" or "somewhat important" — compared with 82 percent of those over the age of sixty-five.[6] The research also showed that the proportion of Jews who married non-Jewish spouses between

2010 and 2020 reached an all-time high of 61 percent. The same survey suggested that less than half of the children from those unions will decide to carry the Jewish banner forward in their own lives, compared with the offspring of two Jewish parents.

On the related question of feeling connected to Israel, 48 percent of eighteen- to twenty-nine-year-olds said that they felt "very/somewhat attached to Israel," as opposed to 67 percent of those over the age of sixty-five.

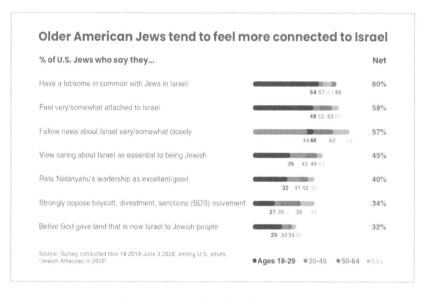

Older American Jews tend to feel more connected to Israel

% of U.S. Jews who say they...   Net

Have a lot/some in common with Jews in Israel	54 57 63 66	60%
Feel very/somewhat attached to Israel	48 52 63 67	58%
Follow news about Israel very/somewhat closely	44 48 62 74	57%
View caring about Israel as essential to being Jewish	35 43 49 57	45%
Rate Netanyahu's leadership as excellent/good	32 41 42 45	40%
Strongly oppose boycott, divestment, sanctions (BDS) movement	27 28 38 44	34%
Belive God gave land that is now Israel to Jewish people	29 33 33 34	32%

Source: Survey conducted Nov.19,2019-June.3,2020. among U.S. adults. "Jewish American in 2020"

●Ages 18-29 ●30-49 ●50-64 ●65+

Pew Research Center data on Jewish Americans, survey conducted Nov. 19, 2019–June 3, 2020.

Just as troubling, a poll commissioned by the American Jewish Committee in 2022 revealed that 26 percent of millennial Jews felt it was OK to distance themselves from Israel in order to better fit in with their social circles (the figure is 9 percent over the age of forty).[7] Roughly the same proportion, 23 percent, said the "anti-Israel climate, on campus or elsewhere, has forced me to hide my Jewish identity" — and 22 percent said that it had damaged their relationships with friends.

The prospect that all of these discouraging statistics may persist within our community — or worsen — poses a significant challenge for the Jewish People. Adding to that, there are also signs that small but vocal proportions of the overall Next Gen population have been forming negative opinions about Jews or Israel — or both.

As we will soon demonstrate, the opinions held by both Jews and non-Jews about Israel and Jewish identity matter a great deal. In fact, they're connected, constantly dancing with each other and affecting one another. But this interconnection does not occur in a vacuum. An enormous amount of it is happening online — at a pace that can often feel like light speed. This is why so much of communication and the dissemination of information in today's world has become a race. One of the top media consultants in American politics, Eric Adelstein, put a finer point on it:

> "There is a prism through which most information is offered up for public consumption. And whether it's a candidate, a product, or a brand, it's often a race to be first in shaping that prism and then hammering your message home through creative repetition. The cardinal rule in campaign politics is to define your brand before an opposing force or source pushes an alternate version of it."[8]

In other words, it's a choice. All of us have equal access to the same set of communications tools. And for that very reason, the challenge that Israel and the Jewish community face right now is actually a massive opening.

THE OPPORTUNITY

The great news is that sitting right alongside many of those unhappy numbers cited above, we also see hard data on the Next Gen — Jews and non-Jews — that augur quite well for Israel's future.

If we act.

Our goal with Ethical Tribing is to exponentially increase the number of young people who feel an affinity for or, better yet, develop a love for Israel. To be clear, what we are *not* trying to do is change people's opinions about the politics in the Middle East. Winning that debate is a Herculean task and not the focus of Ethical Tribing.

What we are saying is that having a positive *feeling* toward Israel is the predicate for having an open mind about the more complex issues that invariably surround it. Context matters in any exchange — but only if context is considered. And we will present empirical proof that makes clear that people have the ability to hold favorable thoughts and feelings toward a country and its people, despite any political beliefs they may have already attached to it.

@**abrokenbackpack** My time in #Israel is already over! I'm keeping great memories – I've met amazing people along the way, ate way too much food (I probably gained 2 kilos in the past two weeks!), appreciated many gorgeous views and tried different experiences. If you are wondering if you should go to Israel and have doubts about the political side of it, simply stop! A country can't be defined only with its political views, there's so much more than that. I felt pretty safe during my time in Israel and I can't wait to be back here!

Melissa Giroux – 67,600 followers on Instagram, Canadian travel influencer, who participated in a travel tour by Vibe Israel in 2018. She returned a year later at the invitation of another organization to speak at an international travel conference in Israel.

https://www.instagram.com/p/BiwldXtn1CF/?taken-by=abrokenbackpack

The great irony right now on American college campuses, and, indeed, across the United States as a whole, is that contrary to the high visibility of noisy protests over the Israeli-Palestinian conflict, most students and young people are not paying close attention to it. Pew Research's most recent publication on this topic in May 2022 reported that 85 percent of Americans between ages eighteen and forty-nine had not heard "much/anything at all" about the Boycott, Divestment, Sanctions movement against Israel.[9]

While Gallup reports that among eighteen- to thirty-five-year-olds, the gap has narrowed between those who express sympathy toward Israel (40 percent) and those who sympathize with the Palestinians (37 percent), nearly a quarter of them do not hold any preference at all.[10] This proportion of undecideds is *over one-third greater* than it is for the next two older age cohorts.

Yet even among young people who have moved toward one side or the other, their opinions are not necessarily fixed for the long haul. Avigail Schneiman, who is the campus student relationship coordinator at the Shalom Hartman Institute of North America, says this is only logical:

> "Frequently, students struggle because they feel they should have both their identity and their positions about the State of Israel 'figured out.' But this ignores that college students are still learning and growing. Why would we ask students to have a formulated position on Israel when they are still trying to figure out the world around them, and indeed their own identities?"[11]

Moreover, there is important data indicating that when the Next Gen is exposed to the truly extraordinary things about Israel — as opposed to redundant political headlines — they warm to the country quickly. And it lasts.

An example that speaks to the power of experiencing Israel in-country is the Birthright Israel program. Founded in 1999, Birthright has taken more than 800,000 Jews between the ages of eighteen and twenty-six (later extended to thirty-two) on a free ten-day trip to Israel. It pulls its participants from 65 countries and nearly 1,000 American colleges.

In 2020, the Cohen Center for Modern Jewish Studies at Brandeis University did an independent study of Birthright's impact on its alumni who had made the journey to Israel between 2001 and 2009.[12] The Center reported:

> "Even a decade after the trip, Birthright participants were about twice as likely to feel 'very much' con- nected to Israel, compared to their peers who did not go on the trip. . . . Participants are much more likely to have a Jewish spouse or partner compared to sim- ilar nonparticipants: 55% versus 39%."

Another educational travel program called Momentum brings Jewish women to Israel from throughout the Diaspora, with the goal of empowering them to "change the world through Jewish values that transform ourselves, our families, and our communities." In its 2019 Impact Report, Momentum noted that after experiencing the program, 76 percent of partici- pants said that Jewish values had become more important to their personal growth.[13] As well, 72 percent increased the number of discussions they had with their children about their global Jewish identity.

So, we do know without question that there are ways to strengthen Jewish identity through sharing the experience of our homeland. The bonus in this equation is that it creates a positive feedback loop: the more that Next Gen Jews who are exposed to Israel and discover that their Jewish identities are bolstered as a result, the more they want to support Israel and share its unique wonders with others.

At the same time, no matter how strong we grow our Jewish Tribe, the fact is that when it comes to changing future perspectives about Israel, we cannot do it alone. We will need non-Jews to connect and engage with Israel to turn the larger tide with respect to modifying attitudes toward the country we love.

Fortunately, attracting and connecting both Jews and non-Jews to Israel is *not* a mutually exclusive proposition. In fact, it's quite the opposite. When we influence the broader Next Gen positively about Israel, it also lends great power to the mission of strengthening our own Tribe's sense of identity.

The statistics we shared earlier in "The Landscape" make clear just how potent peer influence has become in the digital era. So if data are telling us that more than a quarter of Jewish millennials in America feel that it's all right to distance themselves from Israel in order to better fit in with their friends,[14] it stands to reason that if Israel projects a "cool factor" that resonates across the broader Next Gen, young Jews will find it far easier to embrace both Israel and their own Jewish pride. Again, the door swings both ways.

As Jews, we need the entire Next Gen to see all of the beauty, energy, and integrity that make up the true essence of our home country. We need for them to *see what we see* in order to develop their affinity for Israel. We do this by ethically and authentically sharing the values and experiences that we already know are personally important to them.

Of course, we can't just fuel up a grand fleet of jets to transport tens of millions of young people to Israel every year. And if our only other option were to communicate with them through the stale, traditional modes of legacy media, you might not be reading this book.

Thankfully, this is not 1995. Over the past three decades, humankind has gained unprecedented access to information — and formal journalism has been democratized to the point where *anyone* with a smartphone can be a publisher to the world.

This digital reality lies at the core of the Ethical Tribing strategy. We hug it tight. And here is perhaps the best news of all: recent research that we have conducted at Vibe Israel demonstrates just how open-minded and flexible the members of the Next Gen are about how they feel about Israel.

A few months before we began writing this book, we partnered with one of Chicago's premier digital marketers, Hauswirth/Co, and the survey firm Qualtrics. We designed a pilot campaign on Facebook and Instagram targeted toward college students in Atlanta, Miami, and San Francisco.[15] The goal was to discover how receptive a progressive, non-Jewish audience would be to positive messaging about Israel.

The first number that Qualtrics delivered to us was not a surprise: when students were asked what was the first thing they thought of when they heard the word "Israel," 77 percent said either "religion" or "Jewish." In fact, we will be explaining later why those two word identifications are part of the larger branding issue that we're trying to address.

It was the second set of statistics that opened our eyes wide: when asked how favorable or unfavorable a view they had of Israel, a full 40 percent of respondents said they were neither positive nor negative. Blank canvases.

As part of the pilot, we deployed a bilingual digital campaign (English and Spanish) that matched up the interests of Gen Z'ers with Vibe Israel's creative content. The campaign ran for just three weeks, but it substantially moved the needle.

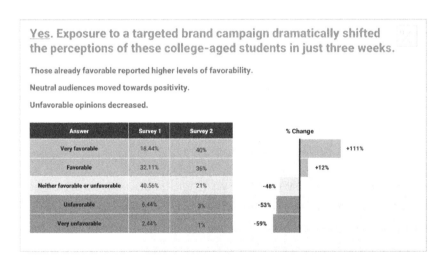

Slide from the Hauswirth/Co report — *Digital Campus Campaigns*

The 18.5 percent who first viewed Israel "very favorably" more than doubled — to 40 percent! Most of that increase was taken from the no-opinion category. At the same time, respondents who started at "unfavorable" or "very unfavorable" — 6.4 percent and 2.4 percent, respectively — *were both cut in half* after seeing the campaign posts.

We will share more detailed information about this research a little later. We preview it here because the numbers so strongly suggest that the challenge Israel faces in how it is perceived is just as much a wide-open opportunity to transform that perception. But it won't happen unless we channel some of that Nachshon-style moxie by exploding the old mold and undertaking a new strategy, unrestrained by conventional wisdom.

The ground is fertile.

HOW TO READ THIS BOOK

As we guide you through the two major parts of this book, out-lined below, we ask you to free your minds and thoughtfully consider this new strategy.

We further ask you not to skip Part I and go straight to Part II, as tempting as that may be. The Parts are presented in sequential order for a purpose. This is how our journey began too: first, we changed our thinking; then, we were open to implementing new actions needed to achieve our mission. We invite you to take the same path.

Part I. Since the start of the 21st century, so much of what the world used to know about communication and social engage-ment has changed. Radically. To be in the right frame of mind to adopt and execute the Ethical Tribing strategy, you will first need to adjust the traditional paradigms in which you have thought about these challenges. In Part I, we will introduce three new perspectives that leave behind the old assumptions and keep us focused on using everything we have learned about connection and persuasion over the past two decades.

Part II. Here we will lay out the six major elements of Ethi-cal Tribing, a strategy based on the sciences of influence and social media communication that is designed to excite and connect the Next Generation — Jewish and non-Jewish — to Israel. Achieving this goal will have a direct impact on the level to which Israel is respected and treated fairly over the long term by the community of nations.

These are the six elements of the Ethical Tribing strategy, form-ing the acronym R.E.S.P.C.T.:

- **Radical Empathy**
- **Emotional Hook**
- **Strategic Storytelling**
- **Pay-to-Play**
- **Crisis Deflation**
- **Track and Tweak**

We will follow Part II with a closing chapter that emphasizes that Ethical Tribing is not a "one-off" strategic campaign; there is no single "election day", per se, when the work of engage-ment ends. As we will explain, executing this strategy suc-cessfully will require a constellation of consistent messaging efforts — and a sustained commitment over time.

———————————

There's an old joke that goes like this: get two Jews in a room and the result will be three opinions. As Jews, we're all in on this gag, because we know how strong-willed, feisty, and downright debate-driven our Tribe can be.

These common Jewish traits manifest every day in the real world. The late former Israeli Prime Minister and President Shimon Peres once expressed it this way:

> "The Jews' greatest contribution to history is dissatisfaction! We're a nation born to be discontented. Whatever exists, we believe can be changed for the better."

In the spirit of our long tradition of ingenuity and endurance, Jews will never stop trying to "change things for the better." It starts with resolutely taking the actions necessary to consolidate and strengthen the fibers of our own Tribe.

We are the ones who will write the story of our future. It has ever been thus. And so let us begin once more.

PART I

NEW PARADIGMS FOR NEW TIMES

1 | The Social (Life) Media Revolution

"Social and digital media is a bullet train, and that bullet train is not coming home."

— Howard Schultz

On a cold, gray Friday in late February 2022, the relatively unknown comedian-turned-president of Ukraine, Volodymyr Zelenskyy, stood in an empty street in central Kyiv, dressed in khaki, military-style clothing, looked straight into his smartphone camera and recorded what would become a historic selfie, announcing:

"I am here. We will not lay down any weapons."

With this simple action, the kind that is taken daily by millions of people around the world — a "selfie" — Zelenskyy ushered in the 2022 Russia-Ukraine war.

You could argue that it was the Russian invasion of Ukraine that launched the war, and you would be right. But what we're talking about is a new kind of war, and with it, a new kind of national leader was born. The kind we will see a lot more of in the future. This was a case study in the use of digital communication to lead a war effort — not just to support it.

Yet importantly, the case study doesn't end there. Whether the goal is to win office, pass controversial policies, manage a crisis, motivate a movement, or dozens of other worthwhile efforts, digital communication through social media is an art that can be mastered to unprecedented effect in the third decade of the 21st century. *Anyone* can play an outsize role in shaping the future, because everyone has the same access to these new modes of outreach and connection.

The ability to powerfully influence others on a global scale using modern communication media has always been integral to success. However, it used to be a luxury afforded to only those at the very top of the social and mainly political pyramid.

We remember Winston Churchill's and Franklin Roosevelt's calming yet forceful voices on the radio during the Second World War. Next came the charismatic and fiery Martin Luther King Jr. and John F. Kennedy in the 1960s, both of whom entranced tens of thousands at rallies with inspiring, often televised speeches that reached millions. And more recently we've watched leaders such as Barack Obama, Donald Trump, and Benjamin Netanyahu, who became masters of the full menu of newer communication tools available to them.

Yet today, anyone who hones these skills, especially through the smart use of social media, can become an overnight sensation on a grand scale. If the songs you write are good enough and you play your guitar well enough, you can upload them to YouTube and become the next Justin Bieber (whose voice is arguably — for better or worse — as influential as some heads of state). And he accomplished this fifteen years ago.

Zelenskyy has undoubtedly emerged as the master of managing a *country's* image during a war, using social media as his weapon of choice. He has turned his words, digital presence, and visible bravery into a silver bullet for inspiring a military that was vastly outnumbered.

Zelenskyy has done far more for Ukraine than bolster his people's national pride at a time of crisis and gain international support for their war effort. The young president has told his people's story on a global scale — with minimal financial investment — and made a positive impression upon millions about his country.

The Russia-Ukraine war is like no other we have experienced before. We watched it in real time, riveted, from front-row virtual seats on our comfortable sofas at home. We witnessed both the terror and the courage that played out simultaneously on the streets of the war-torn country. Think of it as a transfusion of firsthand knowledge — albeit virtual — right into our digital veins, whenever we wanted it. We compared the "humanity" of Zelenskyy and the way he talked, dressed, and handled himself, against the detached, cold, suit-and-tie optics of Vladimir Putin and his comrades. Our feeds filled with viral videos of Ukrainian businessmen wearing khaki T-shirts to show support for their leader, and hip young Ukrainians clearing up rubble of what used to be a housing block, dancing to the tunes of a pop-up deejay.

Yet most of us didn't bother to read about the history of the war (which actually started in 2014), what led to it, why it was happening, and what the context was. We voluntarily exposed ourselves to the unfolding drama on our phones every day, because Zelenskyy and his team were just too good at viral content creation. The result was that our hearts told our heads how to view everything that was happening. And these perspectives spread like wildfire.

THE DIGITAL "BIG BANG"

It's an exciting time in the world: right now, right here, wherever you live, whatever your age, you are part of the greatest revolution since the Industrial Revolution. What you are experiencing and playing an active role in today will be taught in history, marketing, sociology, anthropology, and psychology classes a century from now.

No, we're not referring to the changes introduced by the internet, which burst into our lives some thirty years ago. We might call that the "Information Revolution," in which the human race gained unprecedented access to an almost unlimited amount of information. As revolutionary as that was, it doesn't come close to the next phase.

The title of this chapter, "The Social (Life) Media Revolution," is our term for the exponentially higher level of influence that can be achieved today using a combination of three groundbreaking communication technologies:

1. Social media platforms

2. Smartphones

3. High-speed data streaming

In the 21st century, not only do we have massive access to information — we now have direct access *to one another*. On top of that, we can obtain data about the effectiveness of our digital communication, often in real time, and use it to guide our strategies to enhance future performance.

This "perfect storm" has changed everything. Therefore, by definition it should change the way we think about how to rapidly and effectively connect the Next Gen (most of whom are "digital natives") to Israel.

IS SOCIAL MEDIA A "FAD"?

Before we explain just how key a role the Social (Life) Media Revolution plays in Ethical Tribing, let's pause for a moment and go back about fifteen years.

In 2007, Nokia was "connecting people" with a variety of its mobile phone models. Many of us owned an iPod with thousands of songs (not podcasts yet). On our daily reading lists, we included digital versions of news platforms, blogs, and magazines. Videographers were posting their videos on YouTube, a company that was just two years old at the time. That same year, Apple introduced the iPhone and changed the world forever.

Fifteen years later, we combine the immediacy of human connection that smartphones enabled back then (which is far more advanced today) with the flurry of social communication platforms that were established in the first decade of the 21st century: Facebook in 2004, Reddit in 2005, Twitter in 2006, Instagram in 2010, and we've already mentioned YouTube. The sum of all of this is a major change in the way people are connecting with and influencing one another. Since then, we've been introduced to Snapchat, Instagram Reels, Facebook Stories, and, of course, TikTok.

There's a book by Erik Qualman about how this mega-trend came to be and how it's affecting our lives. It's called *Socialnomics: How Social Media Transforms the Way We Live and Do Business.* In the book and its accompanying video,[1] Qualman confronts an essential question: is social media a fad, or is it the biggest shift since the Industrial Revolution? He offers all kinds of surprising data, but we found this set to be the most compelling:

Years to reach 50 million users:

- Radio: 38
- TV: 13
- Internet: 4
- iPod: 3

Now, consider this fact: Facebook added *over 200 million users — in less than one year!*

That is the Olympic-sprint pace that our world is changing at, and how impactful modern communication has become. The above information is from 2011. Just imagine how quickly TikTok, Snapchat, WhatsApp, and other social engagement platforms have further penetrated our lives and changed the way our children communicate.

Ultimately, Qualman boils it down to a seemingly self-evident — but incredibly important — conclusion:

> "We don't have a choice on whether we do social media, the question is how well we do it."

This is our message to you as well: if we as a community want to connect the Next Generation to Israel, it's not a *choice* between whether or not we are doing social media. **The only questions are: how *well* are we doing it — and how do we *optimize* our performance?**

SOCIAL (LIFE) MEDIA AND WHAT IT MEANS FOR ISRAEL

So we know that social media is not a fad; it's a way of life. Especially for the Next Gen. The game has completely changed.

Anyone who cares about Israel and the future of Jewish Peoplehood must accept that in this new communications age, we don't have the luxury of sticking with old paradigms. We must evolve with the times if we want to usher in change.

In 1985, Steve Jobs told an interviewer that he liked to hire the kind of people at Apple who "want to make a dent in the universe." The reason that quote became famous is because Jobs actually did make a dent every time he introduced a new product.

Just over 20 years later, Jobs made the most significant dent of his career when he introduced the iPhone. In January 2007, he confidently announced to the world: "Today, we are reinventing the phone." Jobs could have said "we are making a *better* phone" — but he didn't. He chose the word "reinventing," because innovating a product of this magnitude required a totally disruptive kind of thinking.

Using this analogy, social media isn't just a *better* printed newspaper, radio, TV, or cable station. It's not even a *better* and more effective website. It's an entirely different beast, because it's not just social *media*. It's also the foundation of the Next Gen's social *life*: it dictates and defines their lifestyle, their choices, their knowledge, and their friendships. In fact, it is a reinvention of the way people communicate.

Since social media *reinvented* human communication, it must be central to the solution we seek, and not just an ancillary aspect of it.

In 2018, Ari Kesisoglu, Facebook's regional director for the Middle East, Turkey, and Africa, said that "people scroll through 90 meters of web content every day — that is the same height as New York's Statue of Liberty."[2] That's a lot of scrolling! We can safely assume that the younger you are, the higher the proportion of that scrolling is taking place on your social media feeds. Older teenagers today surely aren't spending their spare time reading in-depth articles in the *New York Times* or *Sky News World Report,* or a deep-dive study on a Jewish organization's website.

With that in mind, it's no wonder much of their consumer choices, job-seeking efforts, friendship building, development of political affinity, and partner-seeking activities are affected and shaped by social media use. The impact that this new form of communication has had on young people globally cannot be underestimated or ignored when it comes to trying to keep our segment of the Next Gen in the Tribe.

This may seem like a no-brainer, but let's back it up with some facts and figures. For ease of reference, we're going to focus on Gen Z only:

Consumer choices: In 2018, the Yes Lifecycle Marketing company was commissioned by the National Merchants Association to do a study on the buying decisions of Gen Z. They revealed that 80 percent of Gen Z'ers are "influenced by social media when making purchases," versus only 41 percent of baby boomers.[3] Today, it's clear to any brand manager that if you want young people to become fans, you must be on social media, with the right messaging that engages and attracts your target audience.

When we say "any brand," we consider "Israel" to be a brand too. Every country in the world, by definition, is its own brand (we'll go into more of this later in the book). Now, think about it: what are most young people seeing about *Israel* as they scroll through their social media feeds several hours a day?

Political affinity: A survey of 1,000 Gen Z'ers in 2020 done by *Politico* and *Morning Consult* found that they get their news about elections mainly from social media platforms.[4] YouTube was the platform of choice, with 59 percent of respondents choosing it as the one they use "about once a day or more," "a few times a week," or "about once a week." A close second was Instagram with 53 percent, and then Facebook at 43 percent. Twitter and TV followed in fourth and fifth place — with newspapers coming last.

In the context of the topic of this book, this is a serious cause for concern for the Jewish community, many of whom worry about how impressionable members of the Next Gen are and how easily influenced they may be by anti-Israel politicians who are strong on social media. We will touch upon this issue in Part II of the book.

Making friends and dating: "The biggest thing that sets Gen Z apart from Millennials, Gen X, and the Baby Boomer generations is that their relationships have been forming over social media ever since they were old enough to have them."

That quote is from a site called Yubo, which describes itself as a "social live-streaming platform that celebrates the true essence of being young."[5] The observation is based on a research project called "Swipe Right For Love," which surveyed 5,000 college students and found that *91 percent* of them used dating apps.[6] All genders said they used online dating for "entertainment" purposes more than for any other reason.

Gone are the days of courting, writing letters, and getting to know each other on long phone calls. This is the world our children are living in, and these are the social norms they are living by. Which raises the question: how much time do you think they are investing in "making friends with" or "dating" the place called "Israel," based on what they're seeing online?

Job seeking: In a 2019 article at *Inc.com*, Ryan Jenkins, best-selling author and globally recognized millennial and Gen Z guru, wrote: "After job searching and identifying an opportunity at an employer, Generation Z will use digital platforms to learn more about the company."[7] He was relying on a 2018 survey mentioned in the article, which indicated that YouTube was their top platform. Today, it is more likely that TikTok or Instagram would be the go-to.

Why are video platforms the go-to source for Gen Z'ers? Because they're interested in finding out what the specific workplace *looks and feels like*, not just obtaining information about it. Compare this with LinkedIn as the preferred platform for the next older demographic group, millennials, and you start to recognize a complete change in the way twenty-somethings are looking for a job today. For them, a job is far more than something that pays the bills. It's an expression of who you are, where you spend most of your day, the people you interact with — even your value system. Members of Gen Z want to ensure that the place of business that wants them is a good fit for them, first and foremost.

Based on this behavior, we can draw a powerful parallel: analyzing how the Next Gen is changing the way that it becomes part of the workforce is a good indicator for how to successfully connect the Next Gen with Israel.

If we already know that before they commit to a place, they want to see it, experience it in person or vicariously online to feel its vibe, then we must ask ourselves: how much of this proactive engagement is happening when it comes to Israel? Most of what the Next Gen sees online isn't about what the country is really like, or who the Israeli people really are. The sad fact is that the overwhelming majority of the digital content posted about Israel and viewed by the Next Gen on their feeds is about religion and conflict. Can we truly expect this demographic to develop a feeling or desire to connect to Israel based on — and only on — that kind of content to "attract" them?

We could cite many more examples of how social media has taken over when it comes to major (and even minor) life choices — from deciding whether to relocate to another state or country, to choosing which vacation destination to travel to next, to developing philosophical perspectives, etc. Social media is where the Next Gen goes to gather information, get recommendations and advice, learn about new topics, win new friends, and influence other people. Even more accurately, the information comes directly to them. What they see on their feeds is based on the preferences and filters that they have personally defined (as well as the platform's algorithm). It is all centered on their lives.

To this end, it's interesting to take a look at the updated version of Dale Carnegie's bestseller, *How to Win Friends and Influence People in the Digital Age*. The book begins with: "Why Carnegie's Advice Still Matters." One quote in particular spoke volumes to us as it relates to the Ethical Tribing strategy:

> "The two highest levels of influence are achieved when (1) people follow you because of what you've done for them and (2) people follow you because of who you are. In other words, the highest levels of influence are reached when generosity and trustworthiness surround your behavior. This is the price of great, sustainable impact, whether two or two million people are involved."[8]

It is the last sentence that made the most impact on us. Some basic principles of human communication apply no matter what mode we are using. What you say, how you say it, and who's saying it have always been important, whether expressed in person, via broadcast, or now digitally. These principles are still universal today, and they underpin the Ethical Tribing strategy.

After all, isn't this what we're all trying to achieve? To win friends and influence people — about Israel?

@designwanted I didn't want to tell you the story of Israeli design, I just wanted to share the memories of an intense, exciting, unforgettable week. I visited a country that still lies hidden for many aspects and I am very grateful to those who invited me to discover more about it. I lived as one of the locals, I have been to unexpected places and met extraordinary people, driven and confident about their goals. I value attitudes more than competences and for what I can say of Israeli designers, they have a winning soul.

Patrick Abbattista – *Italian founder of Design Wanted, an online design magazine with over a million monthly subscribers, who participated in a design tour by Vibe Israel in 2018. He returned in the summer for a vacation with an Italian friend who had never visited Israel. Patrick, whose magazine is a major sponsor of the Milan Design Week, invited Israeli designers to participate and was willing to make connections for them.*

https://designwanted.com/design-israel/

CONNECTING THE DOTS

Because social media is so central to how the Next Gen operates, and the objective is to connect the Next Gen with Israel, it is our premise that focusing efforts on social media is the fastest and most effective way to succeed. Simple as that.

A couple of final thoughts and takeaways for this chapter:

- Members of the Next Gen are spending more time than ever on social media, and their activity in that space has enormous influence over how they think and feel — about almost everything.

  This means that the proportion of effort and resources that goes into digital engagement with Israel needs to grow dramatically — and fast! Maximizing Israel's positive image on social media lies at the very heart of the Ethical Tribing strategy.

  Some in our community might say: "Wait — aren't we already online? Aren't we on social media right now talking about this stuff?"

  To some extent, yes. But not nearly enough. And not always in a fashion that optimizes the message we're trying to make stick. We all know there's a problem, and the time to tackle it strategically is right now.

- Because the Next Gen has literally grown up on and been substantially shaped by Social (Life) Media, in order to truly connect with them, we must better understand what resonates with them and communicate accordingly.

We cannot take the same traditional approaches that have been used for decades on radio, TV, print newspapers, blogs, or even digital magazines. To achieve the connection with Israel and lasting impression that we seek, we must completely overhaul our understanding of how the Next Gen thinks, operates, and behaves on this medium — and, as a result, in real life.

———————————

The bottom line is that we know there is a solution — an approach that can transform the way young people think about Israel. And it starts with the paradigm shift that recognizes that the Social (Life) Media Revolution is happening and that it's only going to grow in power and influence. It's the place where we need to play — with both strategy and discipline — and there's no turning back.

The good news is that if we board this train and consistently keep it moving in the right direction, we can still win this fight. But to do so, we will first need to shift two more paradigms within our own Tribe.

2 | The Supermarket of Nations

"If you're not making a concerted effort to brand your nation, other people might do it for you — and for their own purposes."

— Tom Lincoln, Director, Wharton Nation Brand Conference

Imagine you're walking into a supermarket. Your shopping cart is empty and the shelves are bursting with products. But this supermarket isn't like the one around the corner from where you live.

Immediately you notice the difference: instead of the "Breakfast Cereals" aisle, you see an aisle called "Travel Destinations." Its shelves are brimming with places to visit around the world: Iceland entices you with a tour inside a volcano; Switzerland offers the Alps and some fantastic chocolate to nibble on while you shop; and New York proudly showcases the Statue of Liberty, as the cowgirl from Times Square prances around in her star-spangled bikini bottoms.

Next up, the "Made-In" aisle is where you may find — out of hundreds of other products manufactured around the world — a car, for example. But what you see is much more than the VW, Mini Cooper, or Lexus cars themselves. You see Germany and its precision and attention to detail in the way the car door shuts and the interior is designed; you see Great Britain and its long tradition weaved into the top-quality seams of the leather seats; and you see Japan's cutting-edge innovation in its gadget-filled, all-electric automobile.

Other aisles parade an array of "Real Estate" deals and "Business Investment" opportunities, "International Sports and Cultural Events" and "Movies and TV Series" to enjoy. There's even a "Universities" aisle, which is particularly relevant for your daughter, who is considering graduate school abroad.

There's an aisle and section for everything in this supermarket, and the choices are endless.

WELCOME TO THE SUPERMARKET OF NATIONS

Here, every product, service, or experience displayed for "purchase" tells the story not only of that brand itself, but also of national characteristics, a lifestyle and spirit of the place that the product or service is from or where the experience takes place.

In the Supermarket of Nations — as in any supermarket — each product tells a story that has to be unique, attractive, and relevant to the shopper, if the objective is for them to grab that product off the shelf and buy it.

People from all over the world shop at the Supermarket of Nations every day. One of the countries they may come across, as they're walking down the aisles that span as far as the eye can see, is *Israel*. Now, ask yourself, would they buy the Israel that they currently see?

It is in this context that we want you to consider how well the product called "Israel" is marketing and selling itself to the world — especially to the Next Gen.

ISRAEL: A COUNTRY, OR A CONFLICT?

The Supermarket of Nations is one of the most competitive arenas out there; every country, region, and city is vying for the shopper's attention at any given moment. In such a reality, we must recognize that Israel is not standing alone on the shelf. No matter the offering (high tech, food, tourism, medical breakthroughs, and so on), there will always be other places that compete with Israel for the hearts and minds of shoppers.

But we cannot ignore the elephant in the room: most places need not trouble themselves with the threats of a well-oiled machine that is consistently claiming they have *no right* to compete on the world stage. But Israel does. This machine is called the Boycott, Divestment, Sanctions (BDS) movement, and we'll be discussing it further a little later on.

The BDS movement has one mission: to recast all perceptions of Israel in the mold of the Israeli-Palestinian conflict. In doing so, in the guise of a human rights movement, its members hope to be rid of Israel altogether,[1] or at the very least to force it into submission to the Palestinians' claims to the land. They are entitled to use this tactic, even if they are playing dirty — for their objective is different from ours. And we must respond; we would be foolish not to.

But we should not let them dictate how we manage Israel's reputation *in its entirety.*

Unfortunately, many within our Tribe fall into this trap, perhaps not without reason. Even those of us who deeply love Israel agree that it has an image problem. Traditionally, the focus has been on directly taking on the anti-Israel narrative and countering it with rational, fact-based arguments. Considering the gravity of the statements being made against Israel, the complementary approach of increasing awareness about Israel's benefits and competitive advantages has been more of an afterthought.

However, this is a surefire way to give the BDS exactly what it wants: if we're investing most of our resources and energy explaining Israel's policies related to the conflict, our ability to showcase the country's most attractive features — in the other aisles of the Supermarket of Nations, where everybody else is happily filling their carts — is significantly curtailed.

The Israeli government and Jewish community's obsession with Israel's detractors is reflected in the size of and resources allocated to the "Israel Advocacy" industry. Hundreds of millions of dollars are invested in this effort, and tens of thousands of admirable foot soldiers are recruited to it every year, ready and willing to fight.

The Hebrew word for "Israel Advocacy" is *hasbara.* Many people use the term, but non-Hebrew speakers often don't know that its literal translation is *explanation,* or *the act of explaining.* In other words, the pro-Israel community seeks to explain the country's complex geopolitical policies in hopes that the world will understand Israel better, embrace its political agenda, and accept it as a welcome member of the community of nations. The assumption is: first you need to *agree* with us, then you will *like* us.

We think it works the other way around. We take our cue from Ambassador Ido Aharoni, Israel's consul general in New York from 2010 to 2016, who is widely credited with introducing the notion of expanding the lens through which Israel's story is told, beyond the conflict. In a *Jerusalem Post* interview toward the end of his term, he lamented:[2]

> "Israel is more than just a conflict, Israel is a real place, it's a real country, with real people, with real achievements, real accomplishments, real aspirations, and we need to celebrate that."

In other words, focusing almost all of Israel's efforts on *hasbara* sidelines the fact that Israel is not a *conflict*; it's a *country*. Israel is there, in the Supermarket of Nations, with hundreds of millions of potential consumers who may be willing to engage with it — if only it offered them something of value that is relevant to their interests.

Most of these people, especially the younger ones, are not spending a lot of time at the "Regional Conflicts" aisle in the Supermarket of Nations, as we will present shortly. They are surely spending much more time in the "Lifestyle" aisles, the "Business" aisles, and the "Travel" aisles, aren't they? This is not to say that Israel shouldn't continue to actively defend its policies and call out unverified, incorrect news and skewed headlines about it. It absolutely should. But is that enough? We think not.

 JOURNEY ERA

ABOUT   PRINT SHOP   BLOG   DESTINATIONS   GALLERY

THE WEEKLY

THE WEEKLY #96: ADVENTURE TRAVEL IN ISRAEL

August 5, 2020 / ISRAEL, THE WEEKLY

@jacksongroves Israel. It's a place I knew little about. In my head, I think I pictured it as a dusty, middle eastern country with a lot of rich history. I knew it was a place of pilgrimage and huge religious importance. However, a few days before I left the Philippines, I asked Nic if he thought it was cold in Israel. We also discussed what food they ate and if it was safe.

One week later and I've eaten a lifetime worth of hummus, seen some amazing natural locations I couldn't have ever imagined and experienced some truly unique moments, places and people throughout my one-week adventure across Israel.

Jackson Groves – 471,000 followers on Instagram, Australian founder of the extreme travel blog Journey Era, who participated in a travel tour by Vibe Israel in 2018.

https://www.journeyera.com/the-weekly-96-adventure-travel-in-israel/

Israel needs to thrive, not just survive, and it cannot do so if people aren't made aware of how much it has to offer beyond the conflict.

To create this awareness, we believe that Israel has to invest heavily in branding and marketing itself. Think of a teen or a twenty- or thirty-something who has no obvious connection to Israel. For them, Israel is nestled between hundreds of other place products, busy staving off its detractors and placing little importance on highlighting its strengths and appeal. How will they see it for all that it has to offer?

Now think of a young *Jewish* person, walking about in the Supermarket of Nations. Israel is there, but will they "buy" it? As we celebrate Israel's 75th year of independence, how shocking is it that the answer is no longer a resounding "Yes!"?

The Ethical Tribing strategy was developed to reignite the desire to connect with Israel that was once a given for Jews. To implement the strategy, we need to view the challenge with fresh eyes and adopt different tactics.

HERE'S A MISSION, SHOULD YOU CHOOSE TO ACCEPT IT

You are hereby appointed the chief marketing officer of Israel (not, by contrast, its attorney general or head of advocacy). Your job is to make sure that the product "Israel" is placed strategically in the right aisle in the Supermarket of Nations, in a prime location, and to make every effort to ensure that it stands out. Your objectives are for potential consumers of this product — Jewish and non-Jewish — to see it, be attracted to it, and ultimately want to buy it.

When you think like a marketer rather than an advocate, the entire playing field changes, as do the strategies, the tools at your disposal, and your metrics for success. And as any marketer today knows, if you're not investing most of your marketing dollars in promoting your product *online*, it will eventually be taken off the shelf.

GREAT EXPECTATIONS

As Israel's chief marketing officer, and assuming you're also concerned about the future of Jewish peoplehood, you'll probably make the strategic decision to go after the *Jewish* Next Gen, as your initial target market.

Before you do, we need to realign your expectations from this demographic.

Prior to the establishment of the State of Israel, when the little Blue Box[3] was passed around, Jews around the world instinctively dropped a couple of coins in it to contribute toward building the fledgling state and safeguarding the future of the Jewish people. Today, when young Jews cannot imagine a world that *does not* include a State of Israel, many Jewish grandparents and parents still assume that their progeny will love Israel, just as they did.

But is that expectation, in the Supermarket of Nations, a reasonable one *today*? With all the competition out there, and so little time and attention, why should our kids and grandkids choose the product "Israel"? And no less importantly — because we can't turn the tide alone — for what reasons should members of the *non-*Jewish Next Gen make that choice?

No self-respecting football coach would make decisions during a game based on a rulebook that has long since changed. This is an apt principle to apply to the challenge before us: Israel and the Jewish communal leadership cannot continue to engage in the same kind of thinking and actions they took at the turn of the century — before the Social (Life) Media Revolution made the Supermarket of Nations even more accessible and competitive — and expect different results when it comes to connecting the Jewish Next Gen to Israel.

It's time for some serious, innovative thinking.

PLACES ARE LIKE PEOPLE; THEY HAVE A PERSONALITY

If you have children, think for a second and try to describe each one in only one word. Joanna, who has three kids, describes her eldest as the "sensitive one," her middle child as the "creative one," and her youngest as the "funny one." Michael, who doesn't have kids, describes his beloved little cousins as the "bold one" and the "sweet one."

Our brains are hardwired to prefer simplicity over complicated concepts. As Israeli Nobel laureate Daniel Kahneman wrote in his bestseller *Thinking, Fast and Slow*: "Laziness is built deep into our nature."[4] Kahneman claims that decision-making is often not a very rational process but rather a quick and intuitive one (our brain does the hard work for us, without our even noticing, but we lose depth of thought along the way). That's why it isn't so difficult to take something as complex as an entire personality and boil it down to one simple characteristic.

We can easily go through a similar process with countries and cities. If we were to ask you to describe the one thing that comes to mind when you think of Paris, we assume most of you would say "romance." What about Brazil? For many, Brazil conjures images of soccer, samba, and the beach. In a word, perhaps, "fun"?

But can places strategically *manage* perceptions about them, and ensure that what people think about them is aligned with what they *want* them to think? The answer, as we will show below, is: yes. And if we understand what other countries are doing — successfully — to manage their global reputation, even through significant public relations crises, then surely there is a lesson to draw for Israel.

PLACE BRANDING: A BURGEONING INDUSTRY

The notion of branding and marketing a place is as old as time itself. The pharaohs branded Egypt with the pyramids; the Romans marched through Europe in uniforms, carrying flags that differentiated them from all others, and built roads that established their superiority; kings and queens throughout history have gone to great lengths to prove their value, using visual cues, policies, and cultural expressions to differentiate their reigns.

Fast-forward several centuries, and as the second millennium drew to a close, several experts in the commercial branding and marketing industry turned their attention to *places* as products. In other words, they realized you can market and sell a country like you do Coca-Cola or an iPhone. They offered their services to governments and municipalities, and these resulted — more often than not — in a dramatic increase in tourism, trade, and investment in these places. By the 2020s, dozens of consultancies and agencies specializing in this field had sprouted, and success stories abound:

Take Estonia's "We Are a Digital Society" strategy, which has turned the cold, gray Baltic state into the new kid on the block of the global tech industry. Estonia's official nation-branding effort, *e-Estonia*,[5] was established in 2016, and by 2021 it was the "fastest-growing nation brand," according to the Global Soft Power Index, recording a 38 percent brand value growth from the previous year.[6]

Or consider Great Britain and Northern Ireland's *GREAT Campaign*, which has not only dramatically boosted the country's economy, but also protected its reputation while it weathered the storms of Brexit, royal controversies, and Boris Johnson's unique style of leadership that cost him his premiership.[7] That campaign, which costs around £60 million a year, brings over £4 billion back into the British economy through increased tourism, trade, and investment.

As the value of these efforts becomes more apparent, more and more countries are establishing official national branding departments to manage their global reputation strategically.[8] The purpose is to boost their economy and national pride, and annual investment ranges from several million to over a hundred million dollars. Here are some ways they do it:

- They offer their citizens guidelines and digital resources to help them share their nation's story with the world, on- and offline.[9]

- They develop multiyear plans to host major sports, cultural and business events, conferences, and festivals, through which their country is discovered by international participants.

- They undertake major policy decisions that are aimed at expressing to the world what they stand for, and act as role models.[10]

- They manage the digital identity of their country so that when people search the country name on a search engine, the *desired* content comes up on the first few pages; and they do the same with social media.

- They invest in training country brand ambassadors from their private sectors,[11] and provide incentives to their businesses to proudly say they are made in that country,[12] so the world knows.

WHAT THE "SUPERMARKET OF NATIONS" MINDSET MEANS FOR ISRAEL

Sustainable place branding is not achieved by a one-off marketing campaign, mega-event or single public policy. Rather, it is a never-ending effort to manage a place's global reputation and share a consistent message about its unique offering, ensuring that perceptions are aligned with reality. Judging by how many countries and cities have established official branding agencies, the burgeoning industry of place branding is shifting from *nice-to-have* to a *must-have* asset.

In 2007, when the notion of place branding and marketing was still new, the *"Brand Israel Project"* was launched by then-Foreign Minister Tzipi Livni and headed by Ambassador Aharoni. But while this kind of thinking permeated the corridors of the Foreign Ministry, and eventually expanded to the Tourism Ministry and Export Institute, the project itself, which depended on multimillion-dollar annual funding for at least five years, did not fully take off. There were a variety of reasons for this, and we hope one day that it will.

In fact, we think it's a strategic necessity, and traditionally, when there is a lack of government investment in a much-needed initiative for the people, for better or worse, philanthropy steps in to fill that void. We are not saying the government of Israel should not be expected to move forward with a national branding effort, but so long as such an effort is not yet fully in place, it is incumbent upon philanthropy and the private and third sectors to take action.

Because rebranding the Jewish homeland and strategically marketing it is not only important for Israel's economy and the national pride of the Israeli people. It also has two more crucial benefits:

1. A strong country brand protects in times of crisis, particularly a public relations crisis. This is crucial for a country like Israel, whose PR crises don't just affect the Israelis themselves; they have a direct impact on the lives of Jews living outside of Israel, too. Imagine, for example, if *Brand Israel*, leading up to the 2014 Gaza War or the 2021 Operation Guardian of the Walls was as strong as *Brand America*'s was when the Guantanamo Bay human rights issues surfaced in 2002 or when the United States allowed any of its states to outlaw abortion in 2022.

2. A rebranding process is a collaborative effort that forces a country to uncover what it does best and defines what its citizens and those who care for it are most proud of.

Finding what unites us and makes us proud of Israel — as the 2009 bestselling book *Start-Up Nation* did, for example — is an integral component of a strong, long-lasting relationship between Israel and the Jewish Diaspora, for generations to come.

CONNECTING THE DOTS

For the product "Israel" to remain competitive in the Supermarket of Nations, we need to think a lot more like chief marketing officers, and a little less like advocates or crisis managers.

- People the world over shop every day in the Supermarket of Nations, where the objective is to highlight a place's appealing qualities and competitive advantages, not just to defend against the naysayers and trolls. Israel, unfortunately, focuses too much of its PR efforts on the latter, and not nearly enough on the former.

- Today, most countries have national branding agencies and organizations, and have reaped priceless rewards from implementing country branding strategies. These efforts boost a country's economy and bolster national pride. If other countries are doing it at this strategic level, why not Israel?

- Adopting a Supermarket of Nations mindset for Israel can do more than just strengthen its economy and increase national pride. Such an effort has the power to heal the rifts between Israel and the global Jewish community, to instill a newfound sense of confidence that Israel has so much to offer to succeeding generations, and, in an indirect way, it can also counter the negative narrative about Israel.

––––––––––––

Ethical Tribing harnesses the power of social media to share a positive, attractive story about Israel, so that it stands out in the Supermarket of Nations. We're almost ready to move on to Part II of the book. But there's one more paradigm shift that our community will need to make before it can put the Ethical Tribing strategy into motion.

3 | The Engagement Ladder

"You can't inspire and lead people without earning their attention. You achieve that in a counterintuitive way — by paying close attention to what interests them."

— Phil Dourado, *The 60 Second Leader*

During the first season of the AMC hit series *Mad Men*, two Israelis from the Ministry of Tourism walk into a conference room at Sterling Cooper advertising in New York. They are accompanied by a cruise line executive, who announces that the group's goal is to turn Haifa into the "Rome of the Mideast." The year is 1960.

Sterling Cooper's dapper creative star, Donald Draper, says it's an "exciting idea." The Israelis pass a copy of the bestseller *Exodus* across the table and explain that it's being made into a motion picture with Paul Newman. Draper accepts the book and jokes:

> "Well, you've certainly saved me some legwork. All I have is the Bible."

Then the Israeli minister of tourism, Yoram Ben Shulhai, replies with a wry smile: "Let's stay away from that." Everyone in the room grins and they share a knowing laugh. The show's audience gets the joke too, because they already associate Israel with religion and the complicated history that is always a part of its present.

There's an easy lesson to draw from this scene: if you're going to interest new people into taking a new kind of action, you'd better present something to them that *they find interesting and compelling.*

And so we've arrived at the crux of our trio of paradigm shifts that are required to embrace the Ethical Tribing strategy. We first talked about the unprecedented power of digital communications in the age of the Social (Life) Media Revolution. Then we broke down how Israel is but one country among a Supermarket of Nations that are all competing for the same, finite pie of tourists, talent, trade dollars, and word-of-mouth support.

Those first two mindset shifts lead us directly to the essential question of this book: how do we actually get them? How do we persuade smart young people to climb aboard the singular adventure that is Israel?

In this chapter, we will answer that question at a conceptual level. Then we will lay out what has been missing when it comes to attracting new people to Israel — and what *is possible* if we start thinking differently about how we communicate with the Next Generation.

STEP BY STEP

Any transaction between individuals, groups, or entities is preceded by a logical process. Whether it's plunking down your hard-earned money for a product, entering into a relationship, championing a new idea or advocating on behalf of a cause, the decision to do so very rarely happens instantaneously. Consciously or not, we all go through a sequential set of steps between the time we are introduced to a potential action, and that moment when we ultimately decide whether or not we're going to take it.

This series of steps has not varied much over the years. It's been known by different names, such as "stimulus response model," "marketing funnel," and "customer acquisition." A more recent iteration of it, which we've tailored to our mission here, is "The Engagement Ladder."

The Engagement Ladder is used in any field requiring the gradual development of affinity for a person, product, place, or cause. A political campaign uses the ladder to gain support for a new candidate. Companies use it to move potential customers from first learning about a product to engaging with it, buying it, and then telling their friends about it. Charitable organizations leverage the ladder to advertise their cause and convert people of goodwill to become advocates for their mission.

The Engagement Ladder is also used by places around the world to generate initial interest and then motivate people into taking action. This may include visiting, buying products, or holding an event there. All of these are actions that almost always come before a person makes a decision to engage in advocacy — and that's the true prize that we seek here.

To be clear, when we say that we're seeking "advocates" for Israel, we're using that word in its broadest form. Advocates are composed of various groups, depending on interest area. First among equals is the group we refer to as "capital-A" Advocates. These are the thousands of noble voices who for so many years — beginning long before 1948 — have made the case for a strong and independent State of Israel with the right to ensure its own security, just as all sovereign states enjoy.

These Advocates are part of the backbone of Jewish Peoplehood. We need them, and we will continue to need them — always. It is one of the reasons we must inspire a love for Israel within the Next Gen, because it is from this new cohort that we will be drawing bold new voices to carry forward the Israel banner. Like a big league ball club calling up players from its farm system, we need to cultivate more members of the Next Gen so that some of them may become capital-A Advocates.

But as we've outlined, as crucial as our traditional Advocates are to making Israel's geopolitical case, we know that this is not enough. **We must attract a far broader base of supporters who will decide to back Israel in ways that are most comfortable to them.** A new Advocate might choose to share posts on their Social (Life) Media platforms. Others may be planning group trips to introduce their friends to Israel. Some may be joining Israeli-led causes, such as IsraAID,

United Hatzalah, Save a Child's Heart, and myriad other organizations that do invaluable work.

Just as importantly, there is no pigeonholing what an Advocate for Israel can be. Every single time we convert another Next Gen'er from a stance of indifference toward Israel to having a positive feeling instead, *that's a win*. People's thoughts and feelings have a big impact on those of their friends and peers. It's the ripple effect; engagement can be infectious.

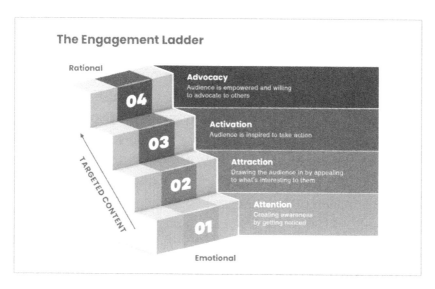

Figure 3.1. The four steps of The Engagement Ladder.

As you can see in Figure 3.1, the four rungs of The Engagement Ladder are ordered very intentionally. And critical to understanding this model is that we cannot get people to ascend to any next level of engagement without having reached the preceding one. There's no shortcut up the staircase.

Several decades before the "golden age of advertising" that was portrayed in *Mad Men,* one of the industry's early giants,

Elias St. Elmo Lewis, became the first to lay out the sequence of steps that would eventually become the spine of The Engagement Ladder. In 1908, print was the only form of mass communication. But that's where Lewis crystallized his first principle, which has not changed to this day:

> "If we cannot gain the reader's attention, it is manifestly impossible for us to interest or convince him."[1]

If it seems like the effort to earn Attention in order to build awareness for a desired action is pretty obvious, you'd be surprised by how many entities out there don't even try. So often, people will put an enormous amount of time and talent into designing and creating a product — but then they'll sit back and wait for consumers to organically discover it. Imagine you've just produced your very first episode of your new podcast. You're thrilled with how it sounds, and you feel great posting it for the world to enjoy. But now you're competing with 2.5 million other podcasts!

While it's no easy task bursting through the deluge of nonstop information in today's world, if you don't get noticed, you can forget about developing any type of growth. No matter what decision you're trying to get your audience to make, *people cannot act upon what they do not know.*

Once that first rung of Attention has been attained for the product or place that we're trying to promote (through advertising, public relations, partnerships, working with influencers, etc.), now we have a shot at rising to the next level: Attraction. In other words, now that we have our audience looking at us or listening to us, are they *liking* what we've cast out into the ether? Does it interest them? Because if it doesn't, that's the second place they'll fall off The Engagement Ladder. If people don't find the information they're digesting to be Attractive in some sense, they will not move further along the path to taking any kind of action. And that's the direction we want this process moving toward.

The last two rungs of the ladder are Activation and Advocacy. Activation can come in the form of liking, sharing or commenting on a social media post, taking a trip, making a purchase, signing up to volunteer — any kind of first-time action that is driven by personal enthusiasm. And if that active experience turns out to be fulfilling, then we've finally opened the door to reaching the highest level of The Engagement Ladder: Advocacy.

It is the first two steps of The Engagement Ladder, Attention and Attraction, that Ethical Tribing is most heavily focused on. They are the 1 + 1 that gets us to the greater sums that can actually move the dial on how Israel is perceived.

But neglecting those first two rungs is actually an innocent mistake that the Jewish community often makes. We assume that our kids or grandkids are already on the edge of the diving board, ready to Activate and take the leap straight into Advocacy. In a way, it's a logical conclusion for us to draw — because that's how many of us have felt. But that doesn't make it true.

If we want the Next Gen to want to become Israel Advocates, then we need them to be aware of Israel's competitive strengths — the incredibly cool, fun, and inspiring things about the country that they will find Attractive and be thirsty to learn more about. We have a unique opportunity to do this right now through the Social (Life) Media Revolution. And once we've intrigued new folks and kept them lingering long enough

Sarah Fennel – *565,000 followers on Instagram, American food influencer who participated in a food tour by Vibe Israel in 2017. This is just one of the responses by readers of Sarah's articles on her blog, showing that they are* Attracted *by Israel's offering. A couple of years later, Sarah served as an* Advocate *by inviting other major food influencers to do a Vibe Tour, which she co-led.*

https://bromabakery.com/the-foodies-guide-to-israel

☰ BROMA 🔍

Laurel.

REPLY

DEBS

MARCH 5, 2017 AT 7:14 AM

Sarah, this trip looks like it was the best! your photos are gorgeous. Israel hasn't really been on my radar as a vacation spot, but this post has made me put it on my list of must visits. Gorgeous!

REPLY

SARAH | BROMA BAKERY

MARCH 5, 2017 AT 1:00 PM

Thank you so much Debs! It was a truly memorable trip, and after visiting, I can't recommend Israel enough! Tel Aviv would be perfect for a summer vacation 🙂

12

REPLY

in our digital aisle of the Supermarket of Nations, that's when it's possible for them to become Activated. To share posts. To talk to their friends. To try Israeli cuisine. To plan a travel adventure.

Sounds pretty simple, right? You might be asking yourself: why wouldn't every country try to do this? Are there real-world examples of this working? What has Israel done? Wouldn't we be the perfect candidate country for this approach?

The first answer is that, as we covered in Chapter 2, most countries do try to do this, and plenty of them have been successful at it. Israel, too, has also made strides in recent years in changing the channel, but it still has a very long way to go in terms of closing the distance between how it is perceived — and the true reality that it has the opportunity to project.

THE GAP

In 1999, an author and journalist named Tina Rosenberg, who for years had been covering the challenges facing countries across Latin America, wrote an article in the *New York Times* with the following lead:

> "It is easy to be numbed by the panorama of violence raging in Colombia. Drug killings, paramilitary massacres, guerrilla kidnappings, death squad murders and street crime have all intertwined."[2]

For many years, and still to this day for many folks, this was the picture of Colombia. It was a perception based to a good degree on reality and furthered by popular TV shows like

Narcos and *Pablo Escobar, The Drug Lord.* But of course the country of Colombia was far more than that.

In 2008, the government agency ProColombia went on the marketing offensive. It unveiled a series of videos that presented to the world the many charms of the country that had been getting lost in all the news chaos.[3] From the Attention it brought to Colombia's vibrant cities, beaches, jungles, music rhythms, mountain regions, and other attractions, a new picture started to emerge. Colombia also centered a campaign on its 1,954 bird species — the most of any country in the world.

At the same time, Colombia didn't try to run away from its tougher realities. In fact, it flipped the script, adopting the slogan: "*El riesgo es que te quieras quedar.*" Translation: "The risk is that you'll want to stay."

The efforts at engagement worked. The most-watched video of the ProColombia campaigns boasted more than three million views. And people began connecting with the things that they liked, which turned into new tourism numbers. Two decades after Rosenberg's article appeared in the *Times*, the same newspaper reported that over three million people had visited Colombia in 2017 — "a 200 percent . . . . increase from 2006."[4]

Colombia, and many other countries that have worked to rebrand themselves, have had meaningful successes in closing the gap between what people's brains have been trained to focus on — through sensational news headlines — and the uniquely wonderful things that each place has to offer. These two realities are not mutually exclusive; it's more a matter of which storylines get emphasized. In other words, there is a competition — a race — that goes on over what representations of a country are going to *grab people's Attention first.*

Israel suffers from a similar brand of perception gap, but perhaps more consistently than any other country on Earth. There is a vast chasm between what people seem to think they know about Israel (a lot) and what they actually know.

We mentioned earlier that when college students were surveyed in 2022 and asked what word came to mind when they heard "Israel," more than 75 percent said either "Jewish" or "religion." This is understandable, as these are two characteristics of a historic nation that every American generation learns about at a relatively young age.

So let's go a little deeper. In 2015, BrandAsset Valuator® (BAV), a subsidiary of WPP, included "Israel" in its ongoing study of 50,000 brands, based on 48 different "personality attributes." The BAV takes input from 100,000 respondents in countries around the world and measures a brand's equity based on four pillars: differentiation, relevance, esteem, and knowledge.

While the good news is that Israel was competitive in the United States with other powerful country brands, such as Australia, France, Germany, Japan, and the UK, there was also a big disconnect: Israel scored higher on *knowledge* and *differentiation* — people's organic impressions of Israel and how they thought it stood apart from other nations. But Israel scored very low on *esteem* and *relevance* — how people viewed Israel's popularity as a brand and its perceived importance to the broader market.

Arrogant
Worth More   Authentic
Visionary   Best Brand
Upper Class   Carefree
Up To Date   Cares for Customers
Unique   Charming
Unapproachable   Daring
Trustworthy   Different
Trendy   The foundation of the BAV model is a set of   Distinctive
Traditional   image, performance and personality   Down To Earth
          variables that have been co-developed with
Stylish   leading marketing academics to quantify   Dynamic
Straightforward   brand identity and brand health. This   Energetic
Socially Responsible   battery of attributes provides the initial pool   Friendly
Social   of potential drivers.   Fun
Simple   These imagery attributes, along with   Gaining in Popularity
Sensuous   measures of appropriateness, regard and   Glamorous
Rugged   familiarity, combine to form the 4 pillars of   Good Value
Restrained   Brand Equity.   Healthy
Reliable   Helpful
Progressive   High Performance
Prestigious   High Quality
Original   Independent
Obliging   Innovative
Leader   Intelligent
Kind

Figure 3.2. WPP's "BrandAsset Valuator®" is based on forty-eight "image, performance, and personality" variables.

In other words, the things that came to people's minds in terms of what they "know" about Israel (Jewish, religion, conflict, strong military) did not make it *Attractive* to them. The BAV study reported that Americans do not "see themselves in Israel" and don't find it to be a very approachable country:

> "Israel's distant persona is a barrier to growth in relevance, which is the driver of Engagement and an indicator of how connected Americans feel to Israel."

We should note that in the absence of a strong and sustained marketing campaign, it shouldn't be such a big surprise that Israel suffers from this perception deficit. For decades, the capital-A Advocates and the Israeli government have spent an enormous amount of time, energy, and resources to make the case for Israel's independence and right to self-governance in the midst of a seemingly interminable conflict. Ironically, the force and strength of Advocates' messaging keeps people's focus on the very factors that make many folks skittish about looking more closely at Israel. They're good at what they do!

This is the perfect spot for us to reiterate that traditional, capital-A pro-Israel Advocacy and the Ethical Tribing strategy are not in competition; they are fully *complementary*. They exist in separate lanes, like two Olympic racers competing on behalf of their country in different sports in different stadiums. Same uniform, same ultimate goal, with each contributing points that get summed up and appear in the international medal standings.

Ironically, the great news for Ethical Tribing from the BAV study is that a whole bunch of dimensions where Israel did not excel in terms of governance are also precisely the areas where Israel does excel in reality! If you know Israel, then you know that a great many of the BAV "personality attributes" shown in Figure 3.2 apply.

These BAV descriptors are tremendously important, because they drive "Relevance." And this is why we need to strategically widen the lens through which the Next Gen views Israel. Again, it is a matter of where we are able to focus their Attention on rung one of The Engagement Ladder, in order to move them up to Attraction on rung two.

Over the past decade, Israel's Ministry of Tourism did receive resources that enabled it to start changing the narrative. In 2019, 4.5 million people visited Israel, and were it not for

COVID-19's impact on tourism, the country would likely have welcomed its 5 millionth visitor in 2020. While this was a substantial increase from the 750,000 it drew twenty years earlier, specialists and professionals in the industry claim that Israel has still barely scratched the surface in terms of its potential to Attract new people, talent, and investment.[5]

At the top of this section, we shared the story of Colombia's successful turnaround. One might counter that Colombia had the advantage of moving past much of its highly publicized military conflict and cartel violence before the growth that accompanied its new marketing efforts. This is a logical point, just as it would be if we applied it to countries like Croatia, Rwanda, and others that were able to leave behind their most recent and visible troubles as they launched successful turnarounds.

These narratives might suggest that because of the deeply complicated conflict Israel is engaged in, which at times can feel eternal, it might be far more difficult to shape people's perceptions of the country. But we already know that Israel has been successful in drawing Attention to — and Attracting new interest in — multiple sectors of its economy. From start-up companies to cutting-edge health care solutions to tech innovations and other success stories, Israel has shown its ability to break through the noise when there is the intent to do so.

One of the best examples of this is the 2009 book *Start-Up Nation: The Story of Israel's Economic Miracle,* by Dan Senor and Saul Singer, which has been translated into twenty languages and made an indelible imprint on the world's view of entrepreneurship in Israel.

Another example is the dazzling photo essay in the *New York Times* declaring Tel Aviv "The Capital of Mediterranean Cool," highlighting its beautiful urban beaches, vibrant cafes and shopping, quaint seaside ports, and "golden hued restaurants."[6]

So even if the controversial circumstances that are a part of Israel make it harder at times to change the subject, this is only another reason to *start changing the subject*. Like our fictional friend Don Draper once said: "If you don't like what's being said, change the conversation."

We must make our efforts to tell Israel's story just as relentless as the flow of messages about its politics that the Next Gen receives through various media filters. The fact that this challenge is in some ways daunting only makes it all the more important to get off the blocks right now. And to never stop.

Though it may not seem self-evident, there is a universe of young people out there who are just waiting to be coaxed up The Engagement Ladder to connect with the real Israel. We must go after every single one of them.

CONNECTING THE DOTS

In our third and final paradigm shift, we have introduced The Engagement Ladder. We've explained why and how this disciplined approach is the most effective way to inspire and motivate the Next Gen to develop a love for Israel that is actionable.

We know that there are four steps up the ladder, to be followed in sequential order:

- **Attention:** Using disruptive content and pushing content out there with the aid of digital platforms to grab people's Attention in order to build awareness about Israel.

- **Attraction:** Creatively tailoring messages to members of the Next Gen that align with their interests — making Israel Attractive and igniting their curiosity to learn more.

- **Activation:** Converting Attraction and desire into concrete decisions — small or large — to engage with and experience Israel.

- **Advocacy:** Based on their newfound love for Israel, moving Next Gen'ers to become loyal Advocates who will share their affinity with their friends and express support for Israel when the going gets rough.

As we conclude the first part of this book and take a breath before transitioning to Part II, we cannot overstate how important these three paradigm shifts are to making real changes to how Israel is perceived for generations to come.

Over the past fifteen years, the world has witnessed a Social (Life) Media Revolution that has transformed the way people

— and especially the Next Gen — absorb, consider, and share information. Every hour of every day.

Over roughly the same time span, and in part because of this revolution of modern communications, more countries than ever are vying for people's curiosity, consumption, and contributions. From their travel and trade dollars to their professional talent to their potential citizenship. As the saying goes, it's a brave new world.

When we take these two shifts into account — the Social (Life) Media Revolution and the Supermarket of Nations — within the context of our objective to build new and lasting support for the State of Israel, that's where The Engagement Ladder makes eminent sense. We can't get there without it.

PART II
A STRATEGY FOR THE DIGITAL ERA

4 Tactic 1: Radical Empathy

"You never really understand a person until you consider things from his point of view . . . . until you climb into his skin and walk around in it."

— Harper Lee, *To Kill a Mockingbird*

"I just can't take it anymore!" screamed Peter Laughter, CEO of Wall Street Services, as he opened his intense TEDx Talk.[1] He was recounting a story from when his mother almost drove their family car into a wall — with him, at six years old, at her side and no seat belt to protect him. In a moment of despair, feeling that her life was too hard to handle, Laughter's mother screamed that sentence that became etched in his memory forever.

"A lot of you are probably thinking that she was a horrible mother, but that couldn't be farther from the truth," he told the audience with visible emotion, extolling her virtues and pointing to the many moments of caring motherhood she exhibited throughout his childhood.

When Laughter was well into his thirties, he discovered that his mother was suffering from a severe case of borderline personality disorder, which he explained is a "particularly insidious mental disorder where the person who has it believes — at some core level — that they are broken . . . and when that part of them that is broken is either brushed up against or acknowledged, they lash out, viciously."

Laughter explained that just knowing that his mother suffered from this disorder meant that he no longer had to react to or be hurt by her behavior, because he understood it was just a symptom. "It wasn't personal," he said. That simple shift in his own understanding, and his resulting tender response to his mother's actions, changed everything else, for the better.

The approach that Laughter was able to use with his mother is known in the therapeutic world as "Radical Empathy." It is an extreme form of empathy, which encourages people to actively consider another person's point of view — *even if we strongly disagree* — in order to connect more deeply with them.[2]

He concluded his remarks with the following advice:

> "Radical Empathy calls on us to deploy a sense of curiosity and wonder in combative situations. It calls on us to wonder: what is going on with that individual?. . . . And when we recognize the state of another human being, we're able to see them as a whole person, not just the part of them that's acting out. . . . And when we're able to do that, we're able to empathize with their situation and move things to a different place."

There's a lesson to be learned from Laughter's experience and Radical Empathy about the subject of this book, don't you think? Perhaps those of us who care about Israel don't like to admit it, but by now many in the community are understandably frustrated by the enormous amount of effort that is invested into engaging the Next Generation with Israel, while consistently receiving a tepid response.

But maybe we've been looking at this whole situation from the wrong point of view: our own. Perhaps the way we should be looking at it is from the point of view of the people we're trying to influence: the Next Gen. Exercising Radical Empathy in this context will allow us to do exactly that.

THE SIGN OF THE TIMES

Let's take a moment to consider the times we are living in.

We have just experienced a global pandemic, which has uprooted our social, financial, and emotional lives at a level that none of us — at least those who have not lived through a world war or similarly earth-shattering experience until now — imagined. And while it may feel like it's behind us, doctors and world health officials have repeatedly warned us that new waves may occur at any time.

As a result, our collective emotions are fraught, and remember that this came in the wake of the #MeToo revolution, which uprooted age-old practices and social norms. Concurrently, on a global scale, people are becoming more polarized than ever — a reality that has cynically been taken advantage of by even the least savvy politicians in recent years. Extremists on both sides have been let loose, which has even resulted in new language entering our lexicon, such as "cancel culture" and "alternative facts."

We are living in tumultuous times — for those of us over forty, it is challenging, no doubt. But imagine what it must be like to live through these times when you're in your thirties, twenties, or teens!

All of this is to say that the worldview of the Next Gen is entirely different from ours. Their values are different, their core sensibilities have been shaped by different global experiences than ours have, and the way they communicate and express themselves is different.

If we want to influence them, we first must truly *understand* them. We must exercise Radical Empathy to be able to connect with them and forge a new path together, as we all navigate the next few decades. This is true about anything, and it is doubly true when it comes to connecting the Next Gen to Israel.

SEE THE WORLD THROUGH THEIR EYES

A basic premise in understanding others is to know that their worldview is affected not just by the house they grew up in, their socioeconomic level, their religious upbringing, or their life experiences. There's something much bigger in scale than individual experience that shapes the way we all see the world: we are all a product of the era in which we are born.

Yes, we are talking about those generational differences again. Each generation is defined by a global event that happened when they were young children, which will affect their entire life experience, regardless of where they came from or where they're going in their natural trajectory.

For those born in the first two decades of the 20th century, it was the Industrial Revolution that shaped their lives, their values, their world viewpoint. Think about the Great Depression that began after the stock market crash of 1929. Imagine how that time shaped the understanding of the world of a ten-year-old born in 1920, and how that stayed in that ten-year-old's psyche until they were well into adulthood, even their golden years.

Baby boomers, especially in the United States (born approximately between 1940 and 1960), were shaped by the Vietnam War and the civil rights movement; Gen X'ers (born somewhere between the 1960s and 1980) by the Cold War and the AIDS pandemic; millennials by 9/11 at the turn of the century and the election of the first Black US president seven years later; and Gen Z'ers, by the subprime mortgage crisis of 2007, President Donald Trump's election in 2016, and the influx of social media accompanying all of these events. And, of course, the COVID-19 pandemic.

Within each generation there are major events that mark our times, such as the Kennedy assassination for American baby boomers and the Rabin assassination for Israeli Gen X'ers. There are too many to mention, but all of these shape how people see the world and how they think and act as a result.

In this context, it makes complete sense that a baby boomer or Gen X'er will find it hard to empathize with a millennial or "zoomer" (a term sometimes used for Gen Z'ers). Our brains may be wired the same, but our life experiences catapult us into completely different worldviews. That is the crux of the problem, and why influencing the Next Gen has been so challenging. It's largely because the community is trying to solve a problem using a set of values, core drivers, and basic realities that are entirely different from those of the Next Gen.

And that's why we chose Radical Empathy as the first element of the Ethical Tribing strategy.

SO WHO ARE THESE NEXT GEN'ERS, ANYWAY?

OK, let's say you're convinced, and willing to jump down the Radical Empathy rabbit hole with us. But where to begin? "If they are so different from me," you may be asking yourself right now, "how can I understand them well enough to know what to serve up to them about Israel?"

Every year, major consulting companies and investment firms try to answer that question, by reviewing Next Gen'ers' consumer behavior, analyzing global trends that are influencing them, and trying to tap into what motivates them. All of this is done in order, primarily, to assist commercial companies to know how to market and sell to them better. From Goldman Sachs, which dedicates an entire section of its website to the conundrum,[3] to Deloitte reports on millennials and Gen Z,[4] everyone is trying to truly understand the Next Gen. They are, in fact, exercising a form of Radical Empathy when they're doing so, albeit for a far less commendable benefit than healthier human relationships. But used ethically, these insights are crucial for us, too, in our quest to understand how best to engage the Next Gen around Israel and Jewish identity.

In a nutshell, and by no means representing an academic review of all the resources out there to shed light on the matter, here are five basic values and core desires that currently drive the Next Gen. If you know nothing else, remember these when you're dealing with this elusive demographic:

1. **Authenticity:** According to an article in *Forbes* on the matter,[5] "'Authenticity' has been shown in Gen Z research as a critical element in how they evaluate products and services. Gen Z consumers want to be able to trust the brand, understand what it stands for and be confident that they aren't being sold a bag of goods."

    As we've noted, young people are whip smart. They can smell condescension and they can also sense a sales pitch coming at them before it's even started. When it comes to Israel, this means that using talking points, pamphlets, and information prepared by an organization with a legitimate (and often commendable) agenda is unlikely to work with most Next Gen'ers. They feel they're not getting the true picture of what Israel is really like with just one side of the story. As a result, the Jewish community has in recent years attempted to do the opposite: present Israel almost entirely through its complexities. But this, too, doesn't paint an authentic picture of this young, vibrant, complicated country.

    Israel is a perfectly imperfect country. Let's authentically tell *that* story. Don't fear doing so; young people see faults in many places and don't always run a mile in the other direction as a result. But you have to be honest if you want to reach them in the first place.

Alexandra Baackes – *79,000 followers on Instagram, American travel influencer who participated in a travel tour by Vibe Israel in 2018 and has since come back umpteen times, including with solo women travelers on retreats she leads all over the world. Here she talks candidly about the "perfectly imperfect" aspects of Israel.*

https://www.instagram.com/p/Cf9Lq4curVY/

@alexinwanderland All my @wanderwomenretreats are special to me... But it's impossible not to acknowledge that some take on a special significance. These Israel retreats, first dreamed up in 2018, launched in 2019, postponed in 2020, and postponed again in 2021, have more hours, energy, tears and laughs poured into their eventual rise to life than any other trips I've ever put together. This is a place where I've been both loved and heartbroken, where I've lost and found myself again, a place I once (and maybe still do?) dream of calling home.

This is also one of the most misunderstood places on the planet, just one of the rich tapestry of countries I adore and run retreats in in the Middle East, and it's one I never stop learning from and about. It was an honor to get to introduce it to 27 women from around the world. Some of my friends commented that they could tell, even from afar, that I had FUN on these trips. Sometimes I forgot I was leading them and not on them, ha. (And then a caterer would call and cancel and suddenly I'd remember).

I won't lie — these trips were challenging to create due to many of Israel's cultural quirks. Issues cropped up daily. But what makes this place magical is that the words are barely out of my mouth to my incredible network of friends and contacts here before solutions start to emerge. I told my guests at the beginning of my trips about the word "balagan," which is loosely translated to chaos — and I think in a fun way. I said I'm going to be honest, things are going to go differently than we expected at times, because that's how life is here, and that's balagan, but one thing I can guarantee you is that we are going to be dazzled. And we were. Can't wait to share more.

2. **Diversity:** In a recent survey by Monster,[6] a global leader in job placements, 83 percent of Gen Z candidates said that a company's commitment to workforce diversity is important when choosing an employer.

This percentage is just an indication of what is, for a person under forty, especially in North America, simply a given. When they walk into a room, they subliminally say to themselves: "I expect to see different skin colors. If I don't, something's wrong and out of line with my worldview." Simple as that.

We would even argue that this now extends to what's known as "cognitive diversity," which is the inclusion of people who have different styles of problem-solving and can offer unique perspectives because they think differently.[7] Next Gen'ers don't want to share a room only with people who are *just like them* in every way. They are seeking to be enriched by people who are different from them. Not just because they see this as a moral necessity, but also because they demand more exciting, transformational experiences (more about that below) because of their limited attention span. Now, in this context, think about it: is there another place on Earth with as much diversity — culturally and cognitively — as Israel? Diversity is a foundational component of Israel's story (for more on this, please see Chapter 6: "Strategic Storytelling"). Perfect! It's just what will keep the Next Gen in the room — *if they know about it.*

3. **Activism and climate justice:** Young people will seek *action* when something does not align with their values. They may be viewed by older generations as lazy and are sometimes called "keyboard activists," since their activism is often limited to clicking on "Like" buttons to express their support for a cause. But this is a misunderstanding of this generation that we must nip in the bud. We know differently, because we've witnessed the Next Gen cleverly using digital tools from the comfort of their couches or the back seat of a car to ignite major social movements — and then exponentially expand them.

Millennials and Gen Z are keenly aware of the world they have inherited — especially when it comes to climate justice and sustainability issues. They are angry, and rightly so, that the generations that came before them didn't do enough to protect the globe we all live in. And now they, and their offspring, need to clean up the mess, quite literally. In a 2021 Pew Research survey,[8] Gen Z'ers and millennials were shown to be more active than older generations in addressing climate change on- and offline. While the same research also indicated that they are stopping short of a full break with fossil fuels, it is clear that they consider the issue to be existential.

Most activities that do not include a climate justice-oriented approach are doomed to be disparaged by the Next Gen. Remember this when you plan your next Israel- or Jewish-related event, campaign, mission, or other experience.

And while you're thinking about that, consider Israel's contribution to technological solutions to climate issues. In fact, it's a world *leader*. Now, there's an opening for engaging the Next Gen with Israel, one that the Jewish National Fund, for example, with its sustainability-centric vision for Israel, leverages — smartly and very successfully.

4. **Spirituality:** "Spiritual but not religious" has become a popular tagline, especially among millennials in the past decade, and of course this is seeping into Gen Z as well. A Pew Research survey published in November 2015 revealed that millennials are less attached to organized religion than their parents and grandparents were at the same age (eighteen to thirty-four) with only about 40 percent saying religion is very important to their lives.[9]

Consider, for example, that 81 percent of Jewish baby boomers described themselves in another Pew survey as "Jews by religion," compared with only 68 percent of Jewish millennials saying the same (the remainder, in both cases, defining themselves as "Jews of no religion").[10] This seismic shift may shock the ultra-religious among us, but it is something we must all reckon with — especially when we're thinking about engaging the Next Generation with Israel and with their own Jewish identity (which for many older generations is inextricably linked with the Jewish religion), not just its heritage or culture.

Upsetting as this may be to some, one must accept the reality and adapt accordingly. **Speaking about Israel only in terms of the "Holy Land" won't cut it anymore; we need to expand the lens through which young people see Israel.** In most cases, talking about Jewish values as coming from the Bible or religious prophets does not pique the interest of a fifteen-year-old today as it did for teens in the '50s. So we must see the world as they see it *now*. We must ask ourselves: how can we share the same basic premises, but in a language and a way that they will connect with and want to engage with? The answer is to shift from religion to spirituality, where relevant. Luckily, Israel has tons of spirituality to go around too.

5. **Transformational experiences:** The Next Gen has very high expectations. Remember Maslow's Hierarchy of Needs theory? That well-known pyramid placed physiological needs such as air, water, food, shelter, sleep, clothing, and reproduction as the most basic needs set. Above that are the need for safety, and then to be loved and belong, and then the need for esteem. Finally, at the top of the pyramid, and the hardest to attain, is the need for self-actualization.

   Well, for most Next Gen'ers, their experience has not been one of lacking basic physiological needs or where they had concrete reasons to fear for their safety on a global scale. For most of them, their lives were shaped by parents who put their children's needs before their own. No, Next Gen'ers view Maslow's first and second pyramid levels as a given, and jump right up to the need to be loved, have a sense of belonging, to be appreciated, and most importantly: they want to achieve self-actualization. If possible, all of the time.

   This means that they walk into an event and expect it to be *life-changing*. They want to be inspired, meet new people, learn new things, and walk away feeling they were seen, and enriched by it. That's why another same ol', same ol' event in a Jewish Federation building might not cut it anymore, unless you bring amazing content and dress the whole place up to be Instagram-worthy. The Next Gen are seeking *transformative experiences* that they can post about and share with all their friends. To their credit — they're creating those kinds of adventures for themselves, too.

Fortunately, Israel is one of those places where you don't have to look too hard to find inspiration in every corner. So, a trip to Israel, an Israel-related event, or a social media campaign, has to offer nothing less than a singularly stimulating experience for our Next Gen — if we want them to keep coming back for more.

Of course, there are many more nuanced aspects of how members of the Next Gen view the world that affect their behavior and expectations (work-life balance, racial equality, gender-related issues, and so forth). But you have to start somewhere, and these are the fundamentals.

If you really want to influence the Next Gen, invite a professional to shed more light and provide further insight on Next Gen engagement. Then, start planning your Israel-related activities with these audiences utilizing your newfound knowledge. And try to set aside any frustrations you may have with these young people. Remember, you were once them. Park your political feelings and any emotional points of view you may have about Israel that may differ from theirs, and radically empathize with how *they* see the world. That way, you can give them exactly what they want.

Once you are communicating ehtically and authentically with your community's young adults and teens, they will not only be more likely to be influenced by you; they just might end up thanking you!

CONNECTING THE DOTS

- When you exercise Radical Empathy, you force yourself to see the other person's worldview so that you understand them better and connect with them on a deeper level. We've all seen this science in action — marketers spend millions trying to really understand consumers' beliefs and values so they know how to craft the right marketing message to hook their audience.

- When you use Radical Empathy, you put aside what *you* want to say, or what's important to *you*, and focus on what *they* want to hear and what's important to *them*. All you have to do is make yourself emotionally interested in what the Next Gen are interested in, and you'll find that sweet spot, quickly. As Dale Carnegie famously said:

  > "You can make more friends in two months by becoming interested in other people than you can in two years by trying to get other people interested in you."

———————

Now that we've outlined the vital importance of better understanding the things that are valued by Next Gen minds, we can move on to the second tactic in our R.E.S.P.C.T. formula: finding the topics that speak to their hearts.

5 | Tactic 2: Emotional Hook

"Let's not forget that the little emotions are the great captains of our lives and we obey them without realizing it."

— Vincent Van Gogh

"What we're about," declared a thirty-something Steve Jobs to a wide-eyed audience of eager marketing students, "isn't making boxes for people to get their jobs done — although we do that well. We do that better than almost anybody, in some cases. But Apple is about something more than that. Apple at the core — its core value is that we believe that people with passion can change the world for the better."[1]

The year was 1997, a decade before he introduced the iPhone, and Jobs was preparing the audience to view a new ad that Apple had just launched.

"And so, what we're going to do in our first brand marketing campaign in several years is to get back to that core value," he said. "What we have is something that I am very moved by. It honors those people who have changed the world. Some of them are living, some of them are not. But the ones that aren't — you'll know, that if they ever used a computer, it would have been a Mac!"

Jobs was talking about what became another of those timeless marketing campaigns that take consumers' emotional connection to a company to a whole new level. The campaign slogan, "Think Different," dominated Apple's messaging for a full five years. It succeeded by attracting an audience that was very specific, but also enormous: those aspiring to change the world.

This was a smart move by Apple, because most of us want to see ourselves this way. The emotional hook Jobs was using to attract potential buyers to Apple products was that aspiration to be a better version of ourselves; one that has the power to change the world. To do that, you'll need a Macintosh, Jobs was subliminally planting into the minds of millions.

What Jobs truly understood was that people don't always buy products because of *what* that product does, or *how* it does it. Those are technicalities that can be easily imitated. Most of the time, people buy products because of *why* the company claims to make them, the value they offer, the emotional benefit one can get from becoming the owner of, and therefore associated with, such a product.

Nike, for example, is about "heroism" — with the villain being our own selves holding us back, and the hero is us again, "Just Doing It." Disney offers "nostalgia," and Coca-Cola is about "optimism." We all want to connect to something emotive; we're motivated by something and drawn to something. **The**

secret of Attraction is finding out what that something is, and serving it to you through well-crafted messaging and visuals: from the way the product looks (even the packaging; think of how you feel when you unbox an Apple product, compared with competing brands) to the marketing campaigns that accompany it and the spirit of the company behind it.

None of this makes rational sense — after all, in the case of a computer or cellphone, they are just that: technological tools that enable greater efficiency and speedier results. So the way to get people to *desire* an Apple computer or phone rather than a Dell computer or Samsung phone, beyond the superiority of the product itself, is the emotional connection they feel with the Apple brand over the others.

Decision-making starts in the heart, not the mind, and a multibillion-dollar industry — branding — is based on this very premise, which yields a financial premium. Jeff Dewar, president of the Kaizen Institute, a global consultancy offering competitive strategy guidance to the world's leading brands, provides this sage advice:

> "Change happens in the boiler room of our emotions — so find out how to light their fires."

In this vein, we are suggesting that finding and highlighting the Emotional Hook with Israel that will cause the Next Gen to *want* to ascend The Engagement Ladder we talked about in Part I, is the mission of our community in the 21st century.

SWING STATE OF MIND

Before we delve deeper into identifying that Emotional Hook that has the power to connect the Next Gen to Israel in the digital era, let's remind ourselves of the audience we are dealing with.

As presented in earlier chapters, for the Next Gen as a whole and the Jewish Next Gen in particular to want to connect to Israel, we cannot rely solely on the ones who are *already positively connected to it emotionally*. There are simply not enough of them. Yet the same is true of the opposing group — those who are completely turned off by, or even hate, Israel. They also do not represent the majority in any piece of research conducted on the matter. Who should our target audience be, in that case?

To better understand this conundrum, the situation Israel is dealing with in terms of its image can be likened to American presidential races. There are the solidly red states, which you know will go to the Republican candidate, and there are the blue states, which you know will support the Democratic candidate. Yet, what happens in the months leading up to Election Day? Presidential candidates recognize that they need to split their campaign time and money among *three*, not two, types of states, in order to win:

1. They'll put just enough effort as is necessary into their *safe states*, the ones they know tend to go to the party they're representing. They do this to ensure that their voters come out in droves on Election Day and secure that expected vote.

2. They'll put some effort — but not much — into the *safe states of the opposing party*, if only to give a nod toward their own voters to keep their spirits up.

3. But everyone knows that the most money and effort invested by American presidential campaigns goes to the *swing states*: those states where there are enough swing voters who could go either way and decide the elections.

The same is true about Israel: those who love it, no matter what (our "safe states"), will likely be drawn to *any* positive messaging that is conveyed to them about Israel. Their Emotional Hook was cast long ago, and it holds strong. Those who hate it are the same. It is unlikely their opinion will be swayed by solid arguments or savvy marketing campaigns, so spending most of our efforts on them is bound to reap very limited results.

The Ethical Tribing strategy is based on directly targeting those "undecideds" (Israel's swing voters, so to speak) rather than trying to change minds that are already set. Thankfully, the "indifferent" Next Gen — together with those who already view Israel favorably — represent the majority in *every* survey of perceptions toward Israel, even in countries the pro-Israel community tends to believe are strongly opposed to Israel's policies.[2]

Elie Wiesel once said:

> "The opposite of love is not hate. It is indifference."

We wholeheartedly agree. We are less concerned about those who love or hate Israel, and are far more worried about those who *don't care much at all about it.* Because indifference allows extremism to creep in when you're not noticing. It presents itself in forms that are not as clear-cut as a movement like the BDS, and it reinvents itself in manifestations such as "cancel culture," "alternative facts," and "fake news," the validity of which nobody bothers to confirm. These phenomena are much harder to fight, explain away, or denounce, for they become ingrained in a society's collective psyche.

From this perspective, it stands to reason that if we want to connect the Next Gen to Israel, and we understand that the way to achieve this depends on how they *feel* about Israel, our focus should be on the silent majority whose feelings can still be positively enhanced and swayed in the direction of our choosing, should it not?

CONNECTION THROUGH PASSION POINTS

There's a catch, though, isn't there? If we're going after young people, most of whom currently don't care much about Israel, how do we get them to pay attention to what we have to say? After all, aren't we talking about, well, Israel?

The way to do this is to look for conversations taking place, on- and offline, about topics that young people care about, and bring Israel into these conversations. This approach is the diametrical opposite of insisting that the conversation *start* with Israel.

In other words: *Israel is the backdrop, not the main show,* because the people we want to appeal to don't care enough about Israel yet to stop in their tracks and pay attention to content featuring "Israel" as the main attraction. We haven't yet grabbed their Attention and so they haven't started to climb that Engagement Ladder.

At this stage, what we want from these people — and there are hundreds of millions of them globally — is for them to view Israel like any other country they would be open to interacting with. We are not asking them yet for support, deep engagement, Action, or Advocacy. We merely want to find that hook that will encourage them to be open to starting a relationship with Israel. Once they're hooked, it will be a much easier task to nudge them up to the higher rungs on the Engagement Ladder.

We know this tactic works because we've seen it in action over and over again for decades:

For example, the book *Start-Up Nation: The Story of Israel's Economic Miracle* opened up an angle of Israel that had not yet reached global awareness in 2009, the year the book was published. This was in spite of the fact that Israel's tech had taken off and became a global leader, alongside Silicon Valley, a good decade earlier. The discovery of Israel's strong and resilient innovation-based economy struck a chord — especially with the American public — which was desperately seeking inspiration at a time when it was getting pounded by the subprime mortgage crisis that affected economies worldwide (and which Israel was able to dodge quite remarkably).

The book became a bestseller, as it covered all three bases of a magnetic message: a reason to pay Attention and become Attracted to its content (the Emotional Hook), great storytelling (the book is peppered with anecdotes and stories, written in a journalistic style), and a claim that was backed up with proof (data) that Israel's economic prowess was truly mind-blowing.

Most importantly, the Israeli and Jewish private, public, and third sectors all bought into the story that the book introduced (because it was true, representing — for a change — something to be proud of!), and they celebrated it on a grand scale, turning it into a part of Israel's narrative ever since.

If you were one of those who had a copy of *Start-Up Nation* and gave it to a non-Jewish friend or colleague, do you remember how you felt when they later told you how much they loved it and how they didn't know this side of Israel at all? We believe that that feeling you had back then of national pride, and perhaps a sense of optimism, shouldn't be a one-time thing. There are dozens of other topics and inspirations that are of interest to people around the world, especially the Next Gen, through which Israel can be discovered. We call them "Passion Points," and here are but a few examples:

- **Food:** If you're a foodie, Israel has a lot to offer you, from Tel Aviv having the most vegans per capita in the world; through the bustling, culturally diverse markets of Jerusalem, Tel Aviv, and Akko; to the innovation and originality of Israeli chefs, which can now be experienced firsthand in the hundreds of Israeli-owned and -inspired restaurants around the world.

Evi Aki – *278,000 followers on Instagram, American food influencer with Nigerian origins, who participated in a food tour by Vibe Israel in 2019.*

Evi Aki

Hi there! Welcome to Ev's Eats, my food and lifestyle blog! I'm Evi, a food lover, spice queen, and travel bug who started this blog to bring delicious recipes, travel inspo, and lots of delicious eats.

@eveseats A few months ago I was lucky enough to travel to Israel with, Vibe Israel, a non profit organization inspiring young people about Israel. It was one of the most amazing experiences of my life, and after only spending a few days in the country; it quickly became one of my favorite countries that I had visited… My view of Israel was completely changed, and I got to tour the country though its food and markets as well as through the people. I learned that the people of Israel of love to celebrate life, they love to move forward through education and technology, and they love to live together. An incredibly friendly people who are there to help whenever they can. I truly love this country, and cannot wait to visit again!

https://evseats.com/the-best-israeli-street-foods/

- **Wellness:** Following up on that quest for spirituality we mentioned previously, many Next Gen'ers are seeking a mind-body-soul connection, and what better place to offer that experience than Israel? We're not just talking about mindful moments in the desert and the Sea of Galilee, or eczema patients discovering products based on Dead Sea minerals; Israel's tech is highly focused on technological health solutions aimed at making life better, and this includes mental health solutions, a significantly trending topic for the Next Gen in the post-COVID-19 era.

- **Pets:** The phrase "dog is man's best friend" may have originated in 18th century Prussia, but it is truly personified in the Israel of today. In fact, Tel Aviv has the highest number of dogs per capita than any other city in the world. Surely this is a great Emotional Hook that Israel can leverage to introduce itself to a highly involved audience (take a look at Chapter 7: "Pay-to-Play" for an example from Vibe Israel on how to do so, very effectively).

- **Female entrepreneurship:** A massive area of interest and motivation for 51 percent of the world's population, where Israel can be a role model, leading the way as the country with the most women entrepreneurs.[3]

- **Social activism:** As we already discussed, the Next Gen considers activism to be a core aspect of who they are and what they expect to see in the world. Imagine the potential connection if each and every one of them knew how much social activism and entrepreneurship happens in Israel!

- **Climate justice:** This is another core value, one in which Israel is a global leader in problem-solving technologies in areas such as desalination, desertification, and other clean-tech categories. Inspirational stories about Israelis working to save the planet abound, we all need to tell more of them in a way that will resonate with the Next Gen (for how to do this, see the next chapter: "Strategic Storytelling").

We could go on, but we think you get the gist: find the angle that people are passionate about, that Emotional Hook, and invite them to get to know Israel through that angle. *Not the other way around.* And remember: to remain ethical, the claim that Israel has something to offer in relation to a chosen Passion Point has to be *real.* Otherwise, it's an empty promise, which will be quickly exposed and rejected.

THE POWER OF THE HALO EFFECT

There's a hidden bonus, for anyone who cares about Israel's image, in generating engagement through Passion Points: a fascinating cognitive bias called "the Halo Effect." We are all subject to this kind of bias, which occurs when an initial positive judgment about a person subconsciously colors the perception of the individual as a whole. That initial positive judgment can be related to finding the person attractive or strong, for example, and this perception makes the person *as a whole* more appealing, making it "difficult to revise that impression based on new or opposing information."[4]

The simplest example is observing that someone is good-looking and then ascribing other attractive qualities to them, such as being interesting, smart, or funny, regardless of whether there is any foundation for such assumptions. We all do it, let's be honest. And those who are aware of their appealing qualities leverage them to their benefit, if they're smart.

The good news is that the same bias applies to places, and recent research by Vibe Israel proves this point convincingly well.[5] In 2021, we commissioned research on American perceptions toward Israel. The audience was aged between twenty-five and forty-four and included 2,200 respondents, half of whom were businesspeople and half who were not.

The survey was conducted in August and September 2021, in the aftermath of Operation Guardian of the Walls. Due to the tremendously negative conversation that took place (especially on social media) against Israel's actions at the time, we fully expected to see a negative impact on Israel's image as a result. And initially, we were not surprised: on a scale of 1 to 5, 1 indicating that the respondent thought Israel was managing the conflict very poorly, and 5 indicating that it was managing the conflict very well, non-businesspeople ranked Israel on average at 2.74 out of 5 — not a great result.

Yet when the businesspeople were asked exactly the same question, they gave Israel an average ranking of 3.5 out of 5! In the marketing world, 3.5 out of 5 is considered the "Love Mark," meaning it's where you want to be as a brand, and anything above that is "gravy."

Again, the only difference between the two sets of respondents was their interest area, and so this is a classic example of the Halo Effect at work. The people who were most likely aware of Israel's tech prowess due to the industry they work in, saw Israel more positively in other areas (its handling of the conflict) than those who did not know Israel through a Passion Point.

Now, imagine if you could get more people to connect with Israel emotionally through topics other than tech. What if people fell in love with Israel because they enjoy traveling there, or they can't get enough of our food, or they're intellectually drawn to our medical research and inspired by our social enterprises? The Halo Effect's extension of these affinities into a better understanding and appreciation of Israel's management of the conflict could work in all of these areas, just as it does with Israel's tech appeal. So, what are we waiting for?

HOOK, LINE, AND SINKER

Another beauty of pairing Next Gen Passion Points with what Israel has to offer is that the Social (Life) Media Revolution is spread through pockets of communities that come together online around a shared topic of relevance and interest (in other words, a Passion Point). It's the way the system is built. And because of this, members of these communities can be easily tracked, targeted, and, if a campaign is well executed, won over. Attention and Attraction are easily generated on digital.

Before the World Wide Web descended upon our lives on a mass scale, around thirty years ago, we all hung out and enriched our lives emotionally, intellectually, and socially in physical spaces (and this type of social communication remains very relevant still). If you loved reading, you may have joined a book club that met once a month, each time in the home of a different club member; if astrology was your thing, you would have gone to a local event about it; if you were into football, you'd gather with your friends and fellow fans and watch the Super Bowl together. The converse is also true: if you couldn't care less about gardening, then your best friend who happened to be a gardening fanatic would likely have found it very difficult to get you to join a nearby gardening class, right?

Well, in this respect, we humans have not changed much, even if technology has — exponentially. The internet collects information and offers access to knowledge by segmenting it into categories of interest; social media works the same, more or less, creating virtual spaces of gathering around a specific topic of interest. Whatever topic you care about, you can find umpteen online communities dedicated to it, and access these communities most of the time without any difficulty.

Technology has given us the gift of a playground of Passion Points, where you can meet others who are as passionate about that point as you are. While we're in that playground, our senses are heightened, because we really *care* about what we're discovering and experiencing.

Since everything online is trackable, you can easily target segments of the Next Gen that you want to influence based on their Passion Points, and use great messaging and storytelling to bring Israel to their awareness. You can do this through working with digital influencers, developing brand partnerships with major content platforms, paying for ads on designated social media channels, and investing in disruptive digital campaigns.

The options are limitless, and this represents a huge opportunity for all of us — we, the authors of this book; you, our readers; and anyone else who cares about Israel and the future of the Jewish People — to invite the Next Gen to start climbing The Engagement Ladder and connect with Israel.

CONNECTING THE DOTS

People are led by emotion much more than by reason. This is true in the corporate, commercial, and political worlds, and even in our personal relationships and decision-making processes. By extension, laying the foundation of Israel engagement on an Emotional Hook that stems from what young people care about *regardless of Israel*, and enabling Israel to shine through this topic, is the fastest and most effective way to build long-term relationships between the Next Gen and Israel.

- If we want to see a change on a global scale in perceptions of Israel that will lead to a greater affinity toward it, a significant proportion of our communal effort should focus on the "indifferent" members of the Next Gen. Both Jewish and non-Jewish. The silent majority that does not already have deeply held feelings about it. Numerically speaking, right now there are simply not enough Israel supporters and lovers out there to move the needle. Fortunately, that limited proportion can also be said about those who hate Israel. Our lowest-hanging fruit, perhaps surprisingly, is composed of the "undecideds" — not the positive minority who are already on our side.

- By focusing efforts on sharing Israel's story through Passion Points that large amounts of people worldwide are drawn to, not only will Israel become more appealing to the Next Gen it's trying to Attract, it will also enjoy the impact of The Halo Effect. Appreciation for Israel in the areas of tech, culture, social initiatives, public policies etc., will provide this crucial audience with more context about the country, its people, and their values. This, in turn, will make it easier for them to view Israel's actions in relation to the conflict in a more nuanced, thoughtful manner.

- The Emotional Hook has to be based on a Passion Point that has a large enough online community and is aligned with something that Israel does well and can offer inspiration and mentoring in. The internet and social media are built on communities that gather around a common area of interest, which lends itself beautifully to our mission. This is why we, the authors of this book, are placing such great importance on the digital arena as our recommended platform of choice for the change the community is seeking.

———————————

In Chapter 4, we talked about the need to see the world through the eyes of the Next Gen (Radical Empathy). In this chapter, we laid out which segments of the Next Gen we should be focusing on, and suggested that the way to lead them up the first and second rungs of The Engagement Ladder is through an Emotional Hook: their Passion Points.

It is now time to move on to the third tactic of the Ethical Tribing strategy: Strategic Storytelling, the oldest form of emotional marketing there is.

6 | Tactic 3: Strategic Storytelling

"Great stories happen to those who can tell them."

— Ira Glass

You have likely heard of Anne Frank, but have you heard of Eva Heyman? Eva was a Jewish teenager who lived in Hungary and perished in Auschwitz in 1944. Anne wrote a diary that has been read by millions. Eva wrote a diary too, but the world knew little about her until the "Eva.Stories" initiative was launched on Holocaust Day 2019.

Let's backtrack a little, to put this project into context. In 2016, Instagram introduced Instagram Stories to compete with the success and appeal of Snapchat Stories, which Mark Zuckerberg feared would grab a big piece of his intended younger audience pie. Contrary to standard Instagram posts that don't have an expiration date, Instagram Stories are not only limited in duration (up to 15 seconds), but also disappear after 24 hours. The idea was to take advantage of young people's FOMO (fear of missing out), something Snapchat was doing extremely well at the time.

A couple of years later, with Instagram Stories going strong, budding Israeli director Maya Kochavi and her media entre- preneur father, Mati Kochavi, thought this medium could be a tremendously effective way to make the Holocaust relevant for young people. But they needed a good story to engage a young, mostly disinterested audience.

Together, they pored over thirty diaries of teenagers from the Holocaust before choosing Eva. In an interview Maya gave just minutes before the campaign was launched, she said they decided on Eva because she was "particularly unique in the sense that she was a very modern girl. . . . She had a crush on this boy, who was seeing another girl; her parents were divorced and she lived with her grandparents. . . . So we felt it was very relatable and very authentic to modern-day childhood."[1]

Accompanied by the provocative slogan "What if a girl in the Holocaust had Instagram?," 220 sequential Instagram videos depicting Eva's experiences, from her life as a young girl to her tragic fate, were uploaded in 24 hours onto the @Eva.stories Instagram page. Within a day, the page boasted 880,000 fol- lowers, eventually topping out at 1.1 million.

Eva.Stories has Attracted more than 120 million views since then. The Kochavis followed up with their highly successful Equiano.Stories project on TikTok, which tells the true story of an African boy who was captured and sent to slavery. Eva.Stories and Equiano.Stories are both prime examples of smart, disruptive, *Strategic Storytelling* on digital platforms aimed at young people: a dramatic, emotional story told by an authentic storyteller, affecting millions in a very short period of time.

STORYTELLING WITH INTENTION

Good stories last, and science shows that they are remembered better than facts presented in any other format.[2] In this chapter, we are not going to break down the art of storytelling and wax lyrical about why it is such an effective way to influence people. We assume you already know this. If not, you are welcome to dive into any of the over 30,000 titles available on Amazon Books & Originals when you search for "Storytelling." Instead, we ask you to focus on the fact that we added the adjective "Strategic" to describe the kind of storytelling we're talking about.

Earlier in this book, we challenged you — when it comes to Israel — to think like a chief marketing officer (CMO). Your company's shareholders would expect you, as CMO, to execute a communications strategy, not go out on a limb, react ad hoc to events, or come up with a brand story that fits your own personal point of view. Along the same line of thinking, as the CMO of *Israel*, you must recognize that to sustainably and lastingly engage the Next Gen in the digital era, telling Israel's Story has to be done *strategically*, with a great deal of thought and intentionality surrounding the effort.

To support your endeavor, in this chapter we will offer practical guidelines to the following questions:

1. What is the Israel Story that resonates with the Next Generation?
2. Who should the storyteller be?
3. How can Israel's story be shared for maximum impact?

WHAT'S YOUR STORY, ISRAEL?

"Brand storytelling is no longer a 'nice to have,'" writes Celinne Da Costa, a *Forbes* contributor and storytelling guru. "It is a 'need to have.' . . . Once your audience knows, trusts, and likes you, they will more likely buy from you. At the very least, you'll have created relationships with people who will become advocates for years to come."[3]

The word "relationships" in Da Costa's quote is what is most important to understand in the context of this chapter: what we should all be aiming for is to develop a relationship with the Next Gen that does not begin and end with *one* interaction, as good as its storytelling may be. **Rather, *every* interaction with our audience should be sharing elements of the overarching story of Israel that we know works best to engage this demographic.** But how does one find out which elements resonate?

First, here's where Tactic 1 comes in handy: put aside your own emotions and perspectives, and exercise Radical Empathy to see the world through the eyes of a millennial or Gen Z'er. Second, just like any self-respecting CMO would do, rely on professional, data-driven advice to identify the building-blocks of the story.

In 2010, the Israeli Ministry of Foreign Affairs published the *Brand Israel Book*[4] as part of a wide-ranging and impressive professional country branding process led by Acanchi, a place branding consultancy from London. The brand positioning chosen for Israel was *Creative Energy*. "Brand positioning," according to the *Brand Israel Book*, "defines how our country is different and able to stand out from competitors. This is expressed as a human quality."

Based on this positioning, and the proposition that *Israel energizes*, a country brand story was presented through three distinct, yet connected, narratives: *Entrepreneurial Zeal*, *Building the Future*, and *Vibrant Diversity*. The book included communication guidelines and supporting messages, and was accompanied by stunning professional photography telling an exciting, vibrant Israel story. Some people and organizations followed the ministry's guidelines, and others told a version of this Israel story organically — unaware of the existence of the *Brand Israel Book*.

Eight years passed, and in the absence of any official iterations, Vibe Israel concluded that Israel's story required a revisit and adaptation to a new reality, in light of the tectonic generational changes during the previous decade. To do this, we hired Bloom Consulting, the premier place branding consultancy, which is a data provider to the World Economic Forum and the OECD on perceptions of places globally. It supports the branding efforts of countries such as Australia, Brazil, New Zealand, and Sweden.

Vibe worked with Bloom for six months in 2018, starting with local research among Israel's private, public, and nonprofit stakeholders (including focus groups among Jewish millennials in the United States). We then conducted global research in 13 countries of strategic importance to Israel to ascertain how people aged fourteen to fifty-two felt about Israel.

By comparing local (and Diaspora) data with the data collected globally, Vibe uncovered the gap we referred to in the "Engagement Ladder" chapter: between what we — those who care for Israel — believe and know it to be, and how the global Next Generation perceived Israel at the time (which has not changed dramatically since).[5]

Armed with this important knowledge, the next stage of the process was launched: discovering the "Central Idea" of Israel. In its report to Vibe Israel, Bloom described the Central Idea as:

> "what the Country wants to be perceived for. . . . This 'Central Idea' is the special driving force behind the nation brand. It is not a slogan nor a marketing initiative. It is a 'golden element', an unspoken word that Countries should never communicate, but rather 'be'. It is the first image, idea and emotion prevailing in the Global Citizens' minds when a Country's name is mentioned on the news or by a friend or relative, or when a memory of a past experience is recalled."

Through another series of workshops and validations, Israel's Central Idea was revealed. Bloom Consulting defined it as the feeling we want people to have when they engage with Israel: *ALIVE.*

In the words of one of the workshop participants who had made Aliyah (immigrated to Israel) twenty years prior:

> "Before I came to Israel, I only saw the world in 2D.
> Israel makes me see everything in 3D, and I love it!"

Inspired by the ALIVE Central Idea, which was confirmed as acceptable by all stakeholders, Bloom and Vibe developed three narratives that make up Israel's Story, adapted to Next Gen values and interests:

Celebrating Life: When raising our wine glasses at the holiday table or cocktails at the buzziest bar in town, we Israelis don't say "Cheers" or "Health" — we say "L'Chaim!" (literally "To life!"). For Israelis, life means family, and family comes first. That's why in Israel, it may feel like we're all family — from the taxi driver asking you about your personal life to a businessperson who invites a colleague visiting from abroad to Friday night dinner at his or her home.

Living Together: Israelis hail from a wide range of cultures, heritages, and religions, forming an incomparable mosaic of colors, traditions, cuisines, religions, and languages. On any given day, you might savor Ashkenazi Jerusalem kugel, rock out to Yemenite music, and sip Arab coffee with a Russian engineer. 100% authentic. Our varying beliefs and backgrounds may sometimes result in friction and highlight our dissimilarities, but that's also where our uniqueness lies: we're a society that's like no other, redefining the true meaning of multiculturalism and diversity.

HI! I'M JENNIFER BORGET

@jenniferborget The average family size is bigger in Israel and it's evident families are a priority there. We ate a Shabbat dinner with a beautiful family and sang songs, passed plates of delicious food, and shared stories. It's powerful to think that so many families carry on this tradition every week. I mentioned before that in Mormon culture there's a traditional weekly event called Family Home Evening. Though it doesn't have the same religious meaning, it reminded me of how important a weekly family gathering can be.

Jennifer Borget – 112,000 followers on Instagram, American mommy blogger, founder of Cherish365 blog, who participated in a mommies tour by Vibe Israel in 2017.

https://cherish365.com/10-things-ill-never-forget-israel/

Kelly – Founder

@beafunmum What I discovered in Israel was a curious mix of deep tradition with mind-blowing-out-of-the-box thinking. It would be easy to consider these things incompatible. As I attempt to explain my observations, I would start with family — the importance of family. You see, investing in family is central to life in Israel, and the role of tradition, culture and food are like threads. These things hold families tightly together, creating memories and instilling values that are passed on through generations. It's about relationships. I heard this message over and over during conversations with people from all walks of life: Family, family is important.

Kelly Barstow – 814,000 followers on Instagram, Australian mommy blogger originally from New Zealand, founder of Be A Fun Mum blog, who participated in a mommies tour by Vibe Israel in 2017.

https://www.beafunmum.com/2017/06/how-israel-helped-me-find-my-motivation/

Moving Forward: Yalla! — it's what Israelis say to move the conversation along or get things going. The word comes from Arabic, and it's been fully adopted in Hebrew to communicate that eager restlessness that characterizes Israelis. The modern State of Israel was built on an ancient dream of a 3,000-year-old nation that was and continues to be guided by the need to make the world a better place. That wide-eyed curiosity and optimism coupled with pragmatism continues to serve as our backbone in everything we do, and we're in a hurry to get it done — so, yalla!

Pulling these three narratives together, a single statement was crafted to serve as a basis for *any* story to be told about Israel, if we want it to appeal to the Next Generation:

Israel is an optimistic nation of dreamers and doers, bound together by time and place, making its mark in the world.

As a quick reminder, Israel's founding father, Theodor Herzl, was a *dreamer* (a playwright) and a *doer* (a politician). Motivated by Herzl's vision and what his dreams and actions led to, Vibe Israel uses the hashtag #DreamersAndDoers whenever we post anything online about Israel.

Before we continue, you might be asking yourself: how can I be sure this story actually works to connect the Next Gen to Israel?

The answer is: because we've been using it since Vibe Israel was established, over a decade ago. Initially, we used the *Creative Energy*-inspired story, and since 2019 we've been using the *ALIVE* Central Idea and its accompanying narratives. We carry them everywhere we go and infuse them in every single story we tell about Israel.

With over 1.2 billion positive mentions about Israel online generated by Vibe Israel's work in the past decade, we can safely say that this is the Israel Story that resonates with the Next Gen.

THE ISRAEL STORY MODEL

The process with Bloom was completed by the end of the year, and in February 2019, Vibe Israel presented the results of our global research, and our own Israel Brand Narratives Book, to then-President Reuven (Ruvi) Rivlin at a highly publicized event.[6]

Figure 6.1. Joanna presenting Vibe Israel's Israel Brand Narratives Book to President Rivlin, February 2019. (Photo Credit: Mark Neiman)

That same year, Rivlin's office entered into a joint initiative with Vibe Israel to produce *Hamsa Aleinu*, a yearlong photo exhibition at Ben Gurion Airport, which highlighted the Living Together narrative. Due to COVID-19, which delayed the project to 2021, the exhibit received only 7 million in-person views instead of the 20 million initially forecast for 2020. But fortunately, Vibe insisted on supplementing the live exhibition with a digital campaign that reached over 30 million people in Israel and the Jewish Diaspora.[7]

The Central Idea and three narratives form a model we are sharing with you for how to tell Israel's story. Vibe uses this model for any Israel-related activity, just as we used it to guide us in developing the content to include in the *Hamsa Aleinu* exhibition. It is our North Star, and we hope it will be yours too.

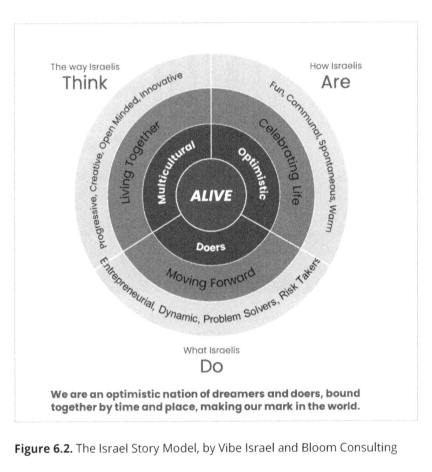

Figure 6.2. The Israel Story Model, by Vibe Israel and Bloom Consulting

How to use this model:

1. The Central Idea — ALIVE — is silent, simple, and not a slogan. It is an *unspoken word* that serves as a guiding light for your communications about Israel. It is how people should *feel* when they hear Israel's Story.

2. In your Israel-related events, social media posts, campaigns, articles, and experiences, make sure you create and curate content that reflects the three main characteristics of Israelis: their multicultural society, optimism, and can-do attitude.

3. To bring Israel's Story to life, use any of the phrases and words that appear in the outer layers of the model to express the Israeli way of thinking, being, and doing.

4. The more often you use the Dreamers and Doers statement, and repeat the words in the model, the stronger they'll stick and become synonymous in the minds of your audience with "Israel."

You can find all of this and more, completely for free, in Vibe Israel's digital storytelling toolbox, accessible through our website (www.vibeisrael.com) and directly at www.unboxing-israel.com. [8]

THE MESSENGER IS THE MESSAGE

Steve Jobs once said:

> "The most powerful person in the world is the storyteller. The storyteller sets the vision, values, and agenda of an entire generation that is to come."

A storyteller has a hefty responsibility, it seems, and therefore, now that we know what Israel Story works best with our audience, we must also ensure that we choose the most *compelling* storytellers to tell it.

Dr. Uri Hasson, an Israeli professor of cognitive neuroscience at Princeton University, is fascinated by what he calls "compelling conversations."

> "You know when you click with someone," Hasson told interviewer Katherine Hobson, who elaborated on what Hasson was getting at: "It's sort of like dancing with a partner; neither person is doing exactly what the other is, but the moves are complementary."[9]

What Hasson was referring to are those truly great conversations you have with someone when "there's mutual understanding and the discussion just flows," as Hobson writes. Some people call it "chemistry." In his laboratory, Hasson studies the mechanics behind conversations like that, and what he has found can serve our purposes extremely well.

Through his research, he discovered that when we speak, our brain waves generate a sound wave — speech — that influences the brain responses of our listeners and brings them into alignment with our own. The more compelling the speaker, the faster and more aligned the waves become. He calls this phenomenon "brain-to-brain coupling" and explains that "coupling is not a result of understanding. It is the neural basis on which we understand one another."[10]

Another Israeli neuroscientist, Dr. Tali Sharot, founder and director of the Affective Brain Lab at University College London, emphasizes the impact of *emotion* on brain-to-brain coupling in her book *The Influential Mind:*

> "Politicians, artists, and anyone with a message to convey are often advised to use emotion to engage an audience. . . . Emotion equates the physiological state of the listener with that of the speaker, which makes it more likely that the listener will process incoming information in a similar manner to how the speaker sees it. This is why eliciting emotion can help in communicating your ideas and having others share your point of view, whether you are conversing with just one individual or talking to thousands."[11]

We should all heed the wisdom of two of the world's leading neuroscientists (not just because they're Israeli!). But just using emotion isn't enough. The storyteller also has to be *authentic,* because authenticity is such an important value to the Next Generation, as we have already explained. **A story based on emotion that is told by an authentic storyteller leads to heightened brain-to-brain coupling and, by extension, to greater influence.**

To better understand what we mean by "authentic storyteller," consider the following scenario:

You're on vacation in Italy, and you've booked a tour of a winery you're excited to visit. The young sommelier, sharing the story of the winery and the excellent wine it produces, does a very good job in conveying the challenges encountered by the family who established the winery over a hundred years ago. He tells stories about the family and shows you the founder's yellowing photo on the wall, and you have a great time.

As you prepare to leave, an elderly woman walks in to bid you farewell. She is the granddaughter of the man pictured on the wall. In a heavy Italian accent, she starts sharing stories of her personal experiences with her grandfather, and then her parents, and now with her own children and grandchildren, as each generation passes down their passion for winemaking to the next. She gives you a big hug goodbye, as if you, too, were her family.

When you go back home and tell your friends about the experience — which of the two storytellers do you think you'll be raving about: the young man or the elderly lady? Each used emotion well, and there was definitely brain-to-brain coupling going on in both instances. But it was probably far more impactful with the founder's granddaughter than the sommelier.

All of this is to say that the best stories — about Israel too — are told by people who have firsthand experience of the genesis of the story, or some personal connection with it. Marketing directors and PR representatives are professional and can be very compelling, but try to find the person who created the invention, came up with the idea, or stumbled across the discovery, to tell the story. They are the most authentic storytellers, because they are able to pepper their story with real-life drama, and their passion will effortlessly shine through. They don't have to be tremendously well-versed in public speaking, and they don't even have to have the best English. They just have to elicit their native Israeli charm, tell an emotional story, and that brain-to-brain coupling will take flight.

STORY-SHARING, NOT JUST STORYTELLING

When we set out to write this book, we asked ourselves: what is the fastest and most effective way to connect the Next Generation to Israel in the digital era?

Why we chose the word "effective" is obvious. We've shown in previous chapters that unfortunately, what has been done to date — though commendable — is simply not moving the needle. Finding the "fastest" way to connect the Next Gen to Israel is the other crucial driver of the Ethical Tribing strategy, because we really do feel that Israel and the Jewish People don't have time to waste. We are saddened to say this, but we must recognize that we are already starting to lose some of our Tribe's younger members because of how they feel about Israel. There is a need for action to turn this creeping tide. *Now.*

Action can be swift in two ways: shortening the time it takes from talking about it to actually doing it, and exponentially increasing the number of people the action affects. If we are each able to influence hundreds of thousands of people or even millions with one action, we will reach our collective objective more quickly.

With that in mind, we recommend a focus not just on story-telling, but also, and just as importantly, on story-*sharing* — in other words, actively seeking ways to ensure that any story being told about Israel that follows the above guidelines is reaching the largest number of people possible.

This is where digital impact and social media come in, big time. Every storytelling opportunity for Israel — whether it be an event, a mission to Israel, a social media post, a magazine, radio, or TV interview, an educational class, etc. — should be *scalable*.

Here are a few ways to reach more than just the direct beneficiaries of the experience:

1. Invite an influencer to attend the event, retweet the story, or interview the storyteller for their blog. Yes, even if it means you have to pay them for it (more on that in the next chapter).

2. Tap into your network of partner organizations and think of creative ways to leverage the opportunity for both of you, thereby doubling your distribution list.

3. Make sure someone is documenting the event professionally (with still photography, and especially vertical videos) and share the experience on your social media platforms, tagging members of your community who are featured in the content.

4. Invest in sponsorship and have the story told as part of someone else's event that you know reaches larger audiences than you can on your own.

5. At physical events, invest in disruptive, visually appealing, designated selfie spaces (in addition to the standard "step-and-repeat" backdrops with your logos all over them), the kind that attendees will think are cool and want to share with their friends.

6. Leave one seat on your mission bus for a micro-influencer from your community who's invited to join the trip for free, and through that influencer enable those who can't come

to experience Israel vicariously, offering rewards for doing so (such as goodies purchased in Israel by the influencer which are then won in a raffle).

7. Work with a professional public relations firm to ensure that stories that humanize Israel appear in local, national, and international news outlets, responding in real time to trending topics of interest to your Next Gen.

8. Invest in paid promotion of content inspired by the Israel Story on the social networks that will reach the exact audience you're interested in influencing. . . .

. . . .The list goes on (and on). This may seem obvious and nothing new, and you're right — it isn't rocket science. But you would be surprised by how many organizations, even large, well-funded ones, cut corners here, don't go the extra mile, and then complain that they are not reaching folks beyond those who are already engaged.

CONNECTING THE DOTS

Stories are remembered up to 22 times more than facts alone,[12] which is why storytelling is a highly effective way to garner Attention and make a message stick. But to truly move the needle, Israel storytelling must be *strategic*.

• The best way to get people to remember anything is through repetition and consistency: tell the same story, over and over, and you have a chance that story will become a fact in people's minds. The Israel Story Model presented in this chapter offers you a clear guideline on what language and content resonate best with the Next Generation.

• Heightened brain-to-brain coupling happens when a great storyteller who is authentic, and uses a good degree of emotion in their story, is chosen to tell the story. Don't compromise on picking the most compelling Israel storytellers to share their experiences with Next Gen audiences.

• Telling a story really well, in whatever format, isn't enough in the era of the Social (Life) Media Revolution. You have to invest creatively in digital promotion — organic and paid — of your Israel-related activity if you want to connect as many Next Gen'ers as possible to Israel, quickly and effectively.

———————

This leads us directly into our next chapter, "Tactic 4: Pay-to-Play," where we will provide you with an overview of how social media works today and why now is not the time to keep your purse strings tied too tightly.

7 | Tactic 4: Pay-to-Play

"You have to learn the rules of the game. And then you have to play better than anyone else."

— US Senator Dianne Feinstein

On International Dog Day (August 26) in 2017, a persistent ad appeared on the Facebook, Instagram, and Twitter feeds of thousands of young dog lovers throughout North America:

"Who wants to go on a Doggy Vacay in Israel?" it read, with a cute, eye-catching image of a dog with sunglasses on, and a little suitcase.

Clicking on the ad led to the form below, which was filled by hundreds of dog owners with wanderlust:

Figure 7.1. Doggy Vacay application form, Vibe Israel.

This disruptive campaign was the brainchild of Vibe Israel, and the objective was to do a different kind of Vibe Tour from the weeklong tours that the organization had begun offering exclusively to digital influencers back in 2011. Every tour Vibe did was generating an average of two million to three million positive organic impressions,[1] but the organization wanted more. With Doggy Vacay, Vibe was looking for a quick win, hoping that *tens* of millions of young people would discover a new perspective of Israel, all within a few weeks.

Why dogs? Because they represent loyalty, friendship, unconditional love, and happiness — all characteristics Vibe wanted people to associate with Israel (because, on a good day, the Israeli people really are all of those things — well, most of them, at least). And, as we mentioned in the "Emotional Hook" chapter, pets are a powerful magnet to draw attention amid all the noise Next Gen'ers are exposed to on their social media platforms.

The six pups Vibe chose to win a spot on the trip were all Dog-fluencers (i.e., dogs who are digital influencers — yes, they exist!). Together, they had a following of 350,000. In late October, the dogs (and their owners) boarded planes in Baltimore, Miami, New York, and Toronto and landed in Tel Aviv, eagerly awaiting a highly customized five-day Israel experience. It was a unique proposition, so they shared their every move, from the moment Vibe declared them as winners with an eye-catching, colorful post, through what they were packing for the trip and, of course, every single minute they were in Israel.

In addition to those who saw the posts by the Dog-fluencers — because they were already following them or because they started following their profiles or Vibe Israel's after discovering posts about the campaign by others online — Vibe also invested in paid promotion, to increase the pool of people who would see the content.

At the end of the campaign, the agency that worked with Vibe Israel presented a formal report that astounded even the most seasoned digital campaigners involved. With an investment of only $24,500 in targeted ads between August 26 and October 27 (when the dogs landed safely back home), the campaign yielded millions of impressions, with an almost unheard-of engagement level[2] of 43 percent — compared with the industry average of 1 to 1.5 percent! Adding to that the impressions attained through organic (i.e., unpaid) reach, the project's overall potential reach[3] was a whopping *700 million*!

@iggyjoey All I want in life is a million treats, a luxury hotel by the beach on the Mediterranean Sea and a never-ending belly rub #doggyvacay. I've applied for a Doggy Vacay with @vibeisrael!

Iggy Joey — voted Canada's top dog model and boasting 79,800 followers on Instagram, applied to win a "Doggy Vacay" in Israel, as part of Vibe Israel's campaign. A few months later, Iggy's owner, together with a couple of the other Doggy Vacay dogs and their owners, were featured at an Israel Bonds event, after Vibe Israel connected them to the Bonds' Young Adults division.

https://www.instagram.com/p/BYJhQTfhIo0

Using social listening and tracking software, Vibe also assessed the *sentiment* of the posts shared about the campaign. This is obviously one of the more important metrics to track for our purposes, especially because we're talking about Israel, a country that regularly contends with a dedicated movement against it. With just 5.9 percent negative sentiment, the Doggy Vacay project is, to this day, considered the organization's most successful, memorable, and impactful digital initiative. It is even the first campaign spotlighted by City Nation Place, the global forum of place branding experts, in its list of "9 Weird and Wonderful Place Marketing Campaigns."[4]

We're sharing this case study to demonstrate the power of paid advertising on social media. Consider the amount spent on the ads — $24,500 — and the number of times the content was potentially seen online — 710,608,240, to be exact. That alone is mind-blowing. But beyond that, social media paid promotion is also highly targeted. Vibe went exactly after the people it wanted to connect to Israel: millennial North American dog lovers, with at least one post-secondary degree, split right down the middle by gender.

You cannot get targeted impact like this using traditional advertising or with organic reach on social media. Even if you're Coca-Cola or Apple, and you have the budget, you are simply unable to target TV, radio, or newspaper ads at this level of accuracy to ensure you're reaching the specific audience you're after.

Marketing costs money, and social media marketing is no exception. Used ethically, investing in advertising to get your voice heard is a wise course of action. Thus, we present the fourth tactic of the Ethical Tribing strategy:

It's a numbers game, with rules of its own. In this game, to reach millions of people, you'll have to reach into your pocket — the deeper, the better — and Pay-to-Play.

SOCIAL PROOFING AND THE RULE OF 77

There is a well-known psychological phenomenon in which people conform to the actions of others under the assumption that those actions are reflective of the correct behavior. There's even a name for it: "Social Proofing." And when social media became a part of our everyday lives, Social Proofing naturally extended itself to this space too.

You probably wouldn't check out a new restaurant today without reviewing what other people have said about it online. And you likely won't hire a service provider that doesn't present any testimonials on its website, would you? It's basic, and it affects all of us, because it rests on a foundational human tendency to follow the pack: if others say something's good (or bad), we often assume this is the case.

A natural conclusion from this, then, is that for Jewish and non-Jewish Next Gen to connect with Israel positively, they need to see and be exposed to positive recommendations about our country and its people. But even that is not sufficient. For Social Proofing to kick in on social media, they need to see this kind of content *over and over (and over) again*.

We know this to be true because of the "Rule of 7," a marketing maxim developed by the movie industry in the 1930s. Studio bosses discovered that potential moviegoers needed to hear or see an ad for a movie at least 7 times to compel them to go see it.[5] This became a hard and fast marketing rule that advertisers abide by to this day.

Fast-forward almost 100 years, and social media now offers brands the opportunity to engage with their users and customers regularly, even daily and hourly. Because there's too much content to sift through, seeing something online 7 times is no longer enough. We think that in the era of the Social (Life) Media Revolution, the maxim should be renamed the "Rule of 77"![6]

When those of us who care about Israel join forces in ensuring that positive Israel content is *constantly* appearing on the Next Gen's social media feeds, Israel will benefit from the desired Social (Life) Media Proofing that will finally move the needle. In doing so, a natural wiring between "Israel" and positive associations — which, for Jewish Next Gen, extends to their Jewish identity — will develop. That wiring will be very hard to break as it becomes etched in the brains of the audiences we wish to influence.

But while in the past, brands were able to create the desired wiring in their customers' minds almost for free, in 2014, all that changed.

THE SLOW DEMISE OF ORGANIC REACH

Facebook's Help Center for business users defines *organic reach* as "the number of people who had an unpaid post from your Page enter their screen."[7] This is just a convoluted way of saying that it's anything you — as a private user — see on your social media feed that has not been paid for to be placed there.

Until 2014, Facebook was totally invested in building its member database, garnering over 1.3 billion users by the end of 2013. To achieve this staggering market share, the social network's algorithm was promoting content by anyone and everyone, as long as it was appealing to a user's specific interests, *for free*. Consumer data equals power, and Facebook was building a treasure trove of data about people all over the world, knowing that eventually it would reap financial rewards from this data.

Facebook users were (and still are) — without even noticing, or not caring much if they did notice — perfectly happy to play along with this. The reason they were so on board with such an obvious intrusion on their privacy was that they wanted to continue enjoying the platform without paying a dime, and if that was the price to pay in order to not have to pay a price, so be it. Such was (and still is) the power of the social need to connect in the digital era.

Mark Zuckerberg could have turned Facebook into a platform with subscription-based memberships (and eventually done the same with Instagram and WhatsApp, which are also now owned by Meta, his holding company). Zuckerberg chose not to go the subscription route, fearing an exodus of users — and other social networks followed suit. But *someone* needs to pay Meta's bills, and if it's not private users of the platform, who else could it be but the business users?

The thing is, businesses also wanted to capitalize on this vast digital billboard (which provided them with consumer data gold as well), and early on they realized they, too, could do so *without paying for the exposure.* An example of this is when a business tags celebrities and influencers in its branded posts.

More and more brands started to crowd the space as a result, which frustrated private Facebook users, who were seeing more branded content than posts by their friends and family. Zuckerberg rightly began to fear that his precious users would leave if he didn't intervene.

As a result, in 2014, Facebook announced a massive change to its algorithm, which from that point on would favor posts by friends and family over branded content *that is unpaid* (i.e., organic). If businesses wanted their posts to get seen, they would have to pay for it. In the words of Rebecca Lieb, a digital advertising and media analyst, "It's a clear message to brands: if you want to sound like an advertiser, buy an ad."[8]

Of course, this was also an extremely lucrative decision for the company, because brands reluctantly adapted to the new rules of the game and started to pay for advertising (which was the only way to continue having access to that treasure trove). Unsurprisingly, as organic reach continues to decline, which ramps up paid revenue, the company's share price increases.[9]

Since then, organic reach has consequently been dying a slow death. In 2018, Facebook once again made a major overhaul to its News Feed[10] to focus less on content from "Pages" (what Facebook calls its business accounts) and more on a user's friends and family updates, which has forced businesses to invest *even more* to get their content seen.

The outcome of all of this is that Facebook and its counterparts have evolved more into paid marketing platforms than ones that are still organic. Layer onto this the fact that Israel, like any other brand in the Supermarket of Nations, is a business, not a private user, and you see why a Pay-to-Play mindset is an integral piece of the puzzle. Without it, unless they're already following accounts relating to Israel, or have friends who are, the Next Gen simply isn't seeing much Israel content on their feeds *at all* — for better or worse.

Allow us to dig a little deeper to hone our point. Worry not, we won't bog you down with technical jargon and algorithmic mechanics. What we're hoping to do is to make it Windex clear that once you know the rules of the social media game, what you must do next, to slightly alter Feinstein's quote above, is to "pay to play better than anyone else."

IF YOU CAN'T BEAT 'EM, JOIN 'EM

On social media, there are only three ways through which consumers are exposed to branded (i.e., not personal) content:

1. **Owned media:** Platforms that the brand controls completely, such as its social media pages, websites, blogs, apps, podcasts, email, and any experience it controls and shares digitally itself.

2. **Earned media:** Content that reaches new audiences through social engagement, press and media coverage, user-generated content (where the brand invites its followers to create their own content about it for sharing purposes), word of mouth, and organic search for the brand.

3. **Paid media:** Ads that appear on social networks and search engines to increase visibility, search engine optimization (to ensure that organic search reaches the brand's owned and earned media platforms), ads for the brand on other digital platforms, paid partnerships with influencers and celebrities, paid referrals and affiliate links, etc.

A *country's* owned and earned media are managed by its government, through official accounts. The Israeli Ministry of Foreign Affairs, for example, has a very active Digital Diplomacy Bureau, with dozens of social media accounts across many platforms.[11] The same goes for other ministries, especially those that are outward facing, such as the Ministry of Tourism.[12] The government invests in paid media, of course, as do municipalities and various other official representatives.

But Israel is not like any other country, and if that were enough, we wouldn't have much need for this book, would we?

We believe that the Pay-to-Play mindset can and must be put into motion *by the entire community*, not just the Israeli government and a select few non-governmental organizations that have already seen the light. Imagine how large our collective budget would be if we all invested in paid media to boost attention and awareness for positive Israel messaging, customized to appeal to the Next Gen. How much quicker could we nudge them up the third and fourth rungs of The Engagement Ladder — Activation and Advocacy — if we all adopted this way of thinking?

To be clear, even though that would be the best route, we are not proposing to pool resources under one umbrella organization and have that organization manage it all. If that had been on the cards for the Jewish People, it would have been done by now (remember — two Jews, three opinions?). But we *are* proposing that every organization involved in promoting Israel positively, and anyone supporting that organization's effort, needs to adopt the Pay-to-Play mindset and get cracking.

We cannot emphasize this enough: without investing in paid media, we will never be able to reach that *proportion of the Next Gen who feel indifferently toward Israel.*

This is because they are not already following Israel-related organizations, and so they are unreachable by those organizations' owned media. They are also unlikely to come across enough Israel-related earned media, unless it is really huge; there's just too much "noise" out there, and they filter out anything that isn't of interest to them. The *only* way they will see the content you want them to see is if they discover it through paid media.

What's more, with paid media, you can use many tools and functions to target your audience more precisely. That said, as of November 2021, targeting users on Facebook by religion is no longer allowed. So to reach Jewish members of the Next Gen, you have to cast a wider net and pay to target a larger Next Gen demographic — knowing that a certain percentage of those reached will be Jewish millennials and Gen Z.

For example, you can target cities and areas where you know these young Jews live or congregate, or colleges they attend, or events they're likely to go to. You can develop brand partnerships with Jewish influencers who have a "cool factor" that extends their influence to non-Jews as well, or invest in having Israel-related content appear in highly popular online magazines that Jewish Next Gen likely read.

With this simple yet immensely powerful tactic, the Jewish and pro-Israel community will *regain control* over what's being shared about Israel online. Gone will be the days of feeling frustrated that all the content we're putting out there isn't making a dent in the universe! Imagine how different the discussions at Shabbat dinner would be, if what your children and grandchildren saw on their smartphones about Israel were overwhelmingly positive.

Every politician, company, and country is using paid media to connect with their audiences. So does the BDS movement. So, if you can't beat them, join them: use the same tactics they use to amplify the positive messaging — and drown out the negative.

CONNECTING THE DOTS

On digital, just like with traditional advertising and public relations, there is an element of investment that is unavoidable. One of the basic components of Ethical Tribing is to adopt a "Pay-to-Play" mindset, because such an investment yields a return that is infinitely greater than any dollar amount spent.

- According to the marketing Rule of 7 (or 77), a one-time digital touch point with anyone you hope to influence doesn't have the power to convert a passive bystander to an active advocate. If you want Israel's Story to stick, you have to get that content in front of the Next Gen over and over (and over) again.

- To actively shape Israel's image in the digital era, you need to reach those who are not following you already, and the only way to do that effectively and rapidly is by heavily investing in paid media.

- If every organization — formal and informal — invested in paid promotion of positive Israel content online, we would have a budget as large as a major company, or even a country. Couple that with what is already invested by the Israeli government and a select few non-governmental organizations, and we have a surefire way of taking back control of the conversation about Israel and shaping it in the manner of our choosing.

We're past the halfway point of our R.E.S.P.C.T. tactics, so it's time for a short recap:

First, we asked you to exercise Radical Empathy in order to understand the audience you're trying to influence. By setting aside your emotions and worldview, and by listening to and trying to think like the Next Gen, you'll be much better equipped to engage with them.

Then, we introduced the power of the Emotional Hook, to explain how you can get the indifferent Next Gen to *want* to engage with Israel.

We also talked about Strategic Storytelling and offered an Israel Story Model for you to use when sharing content about Israel with the Next Gen, so that you are reaching them with a consistent message.

And in this chapter, we explained that targeted messaging needs to be put in front of our audience over and over again, and that the only way to achieve this is by adopting a Pay-to-Play mindset.

We are now ready to move on to our two final tactics, without which the Ethical Tribing strategy won't be complete: Crisis Deflation and Track and Tweak. Are you ready? Because the next chapter is where we show you how to handle, and hopefully tame, the elephant in the room.

8 | Tactic 5: Crisis Deflation

"Sometimes the questions are complicated and the answers are simple."

— Dr. Seuss

We must warn you: what you're about to read is going to sound completely counterintuitive. We are going to make a series of recommendations for how to manage Israel-related social media crises that probably go against everything you're accustomed to. Your visceral reaction may be to dismiss these recommendations out of hand. This is normal: the human brain is wired to automatically disagree with and therefore disregard information that runs counter to what it believes to be true (as we will shortly show).

We are willing to take that risk. All we ask is that you keep reading, nonetheless, as we lay out our case and suggestions. We are confident that it will be worth your while.

The following story is based on true events, but we have changed the names and other minor details for the purposes of discretion:

Katie is a sweet and caring, slightly overweight, fourteen-year-old girl. One day, she went shopping for ingredients to make a cake for her best friend, whose birthday was the following day. She loaded her shopping cart with a variety of sugary products and threw in a couple of chocolate bars and other types of candy.

The cashier — we'll call her Martha — is an opinionated woman with a tendency to speak her mind, even if it is inappropriate. She took one look at all that sugar and unhealthy food that Katie was preparing to buy, another look at the plump teenager, and felt she had to say something.

"Don't you want to take it easy on yourself, dear?" she asked Katie rather loudly. "Maybe you should replace some of this unhealthy stuff with vegetables or fruit that won't be as fattening?"

Katie's face turned bright red; she didn't know what to say, was deeply embarrassed by what had been said and also because other customers had heard it, and ran out of the store, leaving all of the items on the counter. Fighting back the tears, she phoned her mother, Stephanie, who was driving home from a business meeting, and told her what had happened.

Stephanie immediately changed her route to make way to the store to give Martha a piece of her mind, even demand that she be fired! Fuming and filled with understandable rage, Stephanie barged into the store. At the top of her voice, she shouted: "Which one of you is Martha?!" Everyone there stopped shopping and tuned in.

Stephanie walked up to Martha and, in front of everyone, went on a highly vocal, almost uncontrollable rant: "How could you possibly act this way to my daughter?!" she screamed. Stephanie's claims were fully justified, but it didn't seem to bother Martha much. It wasn't the first time someone was offended by something she had to say, and from her perspective, she was only trying to help. Exasperated, Stephanie went searching for the manager of the store. All the other customers were by then paying full attention to the unfolding saga.

———————————

We'll stop our story there and ask you to assume the role of the store manager. You hear muffled shouting through the closed door of your office, and know something's up. How will you handle the situation?

One option is to enter into a public exchange with the inconsolable Stephanie, in front of everyone, so they see you're doing your best. But you also know that nothing you say will appease Stephanie, and, worse yet, some of your customers may leave in protest of your staff's behavior, vowing never to shop with you again.

The smarter approach — we hope you'll agree — would be for you to gently approach Stephanie, recognize and validate her distress, and invite her into your office so that you can both talk about what just happened (preferably behind closed doors). This is not just kind and fair toward Stephanie; it is also a smart move for you. After all, if everyone is busy watching a shouting match that isn't quickly resolved, they won't be shopping at your store anymore. And what if someone started documenting the whole thing on their smartphone?

In the real-life story, the store manager wasn't so smart, unfortunately. Her public, well-meaning yet fumbled reaction (the first option we laid out) did not manage to stop other customers who witnessed the entire thing from walking out in protest.

What the store manager should have done was *deflate* the crisis, not *amplify* it.

"DON'T BE RIGHT, BE SMART"

Unless you are completely oblivious to what goes on in Israel, you, too, felt completely distressed in May 2021, when tensions ran high during Operation Guardian of the Walls. It was infuriating, wasn't it? While Israelis — perhaps even your friends and family — were running into bomb shelters as Hamas, a globally recognized terrorist organization, launched hundreds of rockets at them, it remained a monumental task to successfully sway public opinion in Israel's favor, especially online.

This was exacerbated by the fact that this wasn't an isolated incident. It happens every time: something occurs on the ground in the region, Israel responds somehow, and if you are in some way connected to Israel, your social media feed explodes with vehemently anti-Israel rhetoric, including anti-Semitic undertones that cause Jews worldwide to fear for their safety.

This rhetoric is often led by social media influencers, such as Bella Hadid, who had 56 million followers on Instagram at the time this book was published. Everyone in the pro-Israel community is now convinced that her massive fan base — made up mostly of the Next Gen — is probably also seeing Israel this way. And what about John Oliver and Trevor Noah and what they had to say, from the comfort of their home-based studios? Worse still, some *Jewish* kids are beginning to echo this sentiment against Israel, which is deeply painful for many in the Jewish community.

The community's response? Urgently fundraise to be able to increase Israel Advocacy training for young people on campus and online, set up war rooms in multiple languages to respond to the naysayers, and fight back online with all of the might and resilience its members can muster. The entire community banded together (alongside the government of Israel) and fought a good fight.

But, between us, do you feel Israel won on the digital battlefield?

You probably answered no to that question, and so would we. Why is it, then, that whatever we do, we can't seem to win the PR war for Israel? We, the authors of this book, believe there is a simple yet powerful reason for this, and it is that **social media is the least effective platform to be successful in doing traditional Israel Advocacy.**

Think back to the last time you saw something — anything — that someone said online that you completely disagreed with. Hand on your heart, as your fingers started tapping on your keyboard with a retort, did you have any intention to listen, consider alternative views, and perhaps even have your mind changed? Unlikely. Neither does anyone else. In fact, nobody goes on social media *to be told they are wrong.*

Here's why we stand behind our argument that if you want to be effective in Israel Advocacy, *take it offline*, or at least don't expect high success rates if you're only active online:

First, the most basic requirement for effective human interaction simply doesn't exist on this platform. That is the requirement of *time.* On social media, conversations are taking place at breakneck speed, especially if many people are commenting and responding to one another. You will not be able to shift a person's position — a deeply felt position — in three or four seconds; you need more time. Much more.

Second, people are far more likely to listen to information that is coming from what Dr. Tali Sharot, in her book *The Influential Mind*, calls "an agreeing party" than a "disagreeing party." Sharot recommends[1] a hack for this: find common beliefs or motives that you can connect with the other person over, and that will make them more amenable to a deeper discussion with you. Unfortunately, social media provides you with too few clues upon which to base that *common ground.* You probably know nothing at all about the person you're engaging with, beyond their name and anything they've said in this debate. Sure, you could go look them up, but who can be bothered?

Third, with most optics presenting Israel as the aggressor and the Palestinians the underdogs, you are totally reliant on facts, figures, and credible sources of information to make your case for Israel. However, in the era of "fake news" and "alternative facts," minimal fact-checking even by reliable media platforms, and too many sources of information, your facts and figures can be easily disputed, skewed, disbelieved, and discarded as unreliable. It is very hard to change a person's mind when they don't believe the basic facts you are presenting to them.

Fourth, it has to do with the way our brains work, as this excerpt from a *Harvard Business Review* article[2] explains:

"Conflict wreaks havoc on our brains. We are groomed by evolution to protect ourselves whenever we sense threat . . . . Complex decision-making disappears, as does our access to multiple perspectives. As our attention narrows, we find ourselves trapped in the one perspective that makes us feel the most safe: 'I'm right and you're wrong,' even though we ordinarily see more perspectives."

And it gets worse when it comes to political opinions. Additional research indicates that:

"Challenges to political beliefs cause increased activity in the parts of the brain associated with our sense of self and disengagement from the external world. This may be why people are so resistant to changing their political beliefs. To do so threatens the very idea of who they think they are."[3]

So the starting point on social media when entering a heated debate is: you don't have enough time; you don't have common ground; facts are no longer reliable, news is no longer credible; and our opponent's brain is hardwired to shut down when we tell them they're wrong. It's no wonder we're finding it so hard to win on this battlefield!

But even if you accept this to be true, and recognize that fighting back may be a futile exercise, you can't just abandon the field altogether, can you? At least others, who may not be so negative toward Israel but do see the debate, will be exposed to both sides of the argument? Yes, that makes sense. However, this approach comes at a cost for Israel's image, in the short and long run.

Allow us to elaborate:

We mentioned in the previous chapter that Facebook over-hauled its algorithm in 2014 and that it continues to update it all the time. One of its updates, which it called "Meaningful Social Interactions," gave outsize weight to posts that sparked lots of comments and replies. In other words, when the algorithm detects a conversation with a lot of interaction, it gives it more "airtime," prioritizing it over other content being posted, and pushing it into more and more of people's news feeds who may not be involved but could be drawn in. What started as one person stating an opinion turns into an explosion of people, sometimes thousands, joining the debate. That's why you felt your social media feeds blew up in May 2021. It's basic math.

What this means is that the price we pay for wanting to be *right,* even though we know we're not going to convince the other side, is that we're inadvertently amplifying our detractors' anti-Israel statements and bringing them to the attention of more and more people. Previous chapters in this book have offered guidance on how to use the social media algorithm to Israel's benefit. But it works both ways, and that amplification — more akin to Kryptonite as it applies here — *can hurt us as much as it can help us.*

Finally, there's the issue of what happens once the argument dies down and people move on to the next shiny piece of content. They may have moved on, but the conflict-related content isn't going anywhere. Unlike daily newspapers, digital media's shelf life is indefinite. You can search on Google today and find content that was published twenty years ago. Which means that once the crisis is over, when people are searching for "Israel" — for example, for travel or business purposes — the search results include content that was published during a crisis. So people who search for Israel for reasons unrelated to the conflict end up being exposed to lots of images, memes, and video links, about Israel *and* the conflict, long after the crisis is over.

Bear in mind that most of this content was published by. . . . the pro-Israel community and well-meaning Israel Advocates! We're talking about those eye-catching memes we shared that said: *"In the last hour, 200 rockets have been launched against Israel by the Hamas terrorist organization,"* or that famous video of the Iron Dome in action.[4] Imagine the impression this makes on a random person considering Israel as their next travel destination or business investment!

We know we can't control what Bella Hadid or anyone else who is anti-Israel is sharing. But we certainly *can* control what *we* upload. The next time you share an image or video that's related to a military operation taking place, we hope you will think twice about this and perhaps reconsider.

In summary, we are recommending to literally take a page out of the Bible and heed the counterintuitive advice offered to Moses by Jethro, from the weekly Torah portion bearing his name: *"Don't be right,"* Jethro said to Moses. *"Be smart."*

NOW WHAT?

If you care for Israel, you must be asking yourself at this point: "OK, fine, I'm convinced. But what *can* I do? Surely, you're not expecting me to sit back and do nothing while Israel's name is being tarnished? While anti-Zionism and anti-Semitism are conflated and now I fear for my family's physical safety, thousands of miles away from Israel!"

No, of course we're not.

Here's what we propose to do the next time there's any action relating to Israel that sparks another social media frenzy:

1. **Don't engage, publicly.** When you see negative comments about Israel, *don't respond*. There, we said it and it is the most counterintuitive thing you'll read in this entire book. But let this statement linger for a moment: there really is no point in engaging because you likely won't win the debate, for all the reasons we listed above. And because it takes two to tango, if you don't respond, the algorithm won't detect increased interaction and the shelf life of the statements shared by the naysayers will start to expire. Eventually, the noise they make will die off and disappear much faster. It's a simple solution to a complicated problem.

   And always keep in mind, we have professionals who are countering the inaccuracies and falsehoods and clearly stating Israel's case. Ambassadors, federal officeholders and highly respected opinion leaders are communicating both on high profile media platforms and in the corridors of power where consequential decision-making takes place. As well, we have community professionals who are actively pushing the social media companies to regulate content and to diminish anti-Semitic and anti-Zionist rhetoric — often with real success. Rest assured, a fight is being waged; at no time is there a void of our voice.

2. **Do engage, privately.** Since we know that you may not be able to abide doing nothing, what you *can* do is look for those people who are participating in the exchange but don't

appear to be anti-Semitic or completely closed to having a deeper conversation, and invite them to discuss the matter privately by pinging them a friendly message via the social platform you're both engaging on. The language you use should be non-combative and inviting, along the lines of: *"Hey [first name], I've been following the discussion in response to [post author's name]'s post, and saw what you wrote. I'm interested in hearing your thoughts on this matter. Can we have a conversation here?"* Then, muster all the self-control you have and quietly wait for the other person to respond. If they do, you can start engaging them in a deeper conversation about the situation (see the next bullet point for advice on how), and you may even get them to see your point of view. But don't become frustrated with them if they don't. It takes time; Rome wasn't built in a day. If nothing else, they may walk away from the conversation feeling heard and validated. Not a bad result, all things considered.

3. **Use persuasion and influence tactics.** Dale Carnegie's first rule is: *never criticize, condemn, or complain*.[5] Most of us, at least when faced with someone we think is completely wrong about Israel, fail to follow Carnegie's sage advice. We vilify people we disagree with, call out their stupidity, and give as good as we get. But that won't get us what we want, will it? So, if you want someone who you're deeply disagreeing with to listen to you, try to approach them in a respectful, more validating manner. There are a variety of tactics to use, and Vibe Israel partnered with Ariel Halevi, a specialist in persuasion and influence, to offer a free online course that teaches these tactics in under ninety minutes. We even have a course on how to talk to your teenager about Israel.[6]

Interaction between Pakistani anti-Zionist and Joanna

In response to an anti-Israel post by someone on LinkedIn, a Pakistani engineer wrote that *"All Israelis hate Muslims."* Joanna, while writing this chapter, thought she'd try out our own advice. She answered in a comment (publicly):

"Hi Daud, if all I saw about Israel on my feed was this kind of content, I'd probably feel the same. I was just wondering: where do you get this information from — that all Israelis hate Muslims?"

Daud commented back:

"If I'm wrong, prove it."

Joanna wanted to respond publicly and provide him with proof, but recognized that Daud would likely not change his mind very quickly and that this was going to take a while. So she took a deep breath and sent him a private, respectful message instead. Here's how it turned out.

Daud did not become pro-Israel, but if Joanna were to continue interacting with him over time, he may well have become less anti-Zionist. Most importantly, this interaction, which lasted a couple more posts between Joanna and Daud, was kept out of the public sphere, and therefore didn't indicate to the algorithm of LinkedIn to promote the conversation.

Joanna Landau 1:32 · **ג'ואנה לנדאו** PM

Hi, I'm not claiming either way. I'm just wondering where you get information that causes you to conclude that Israelis by definition hate Muslims? It just seems like quite a generalization, and I live in Israel and don't see it so was wondering. I'm sure there are extremists on either side, like anywhere.

Daud ▉▉▉ 1:39 PM

You can see lots of posts, internet is full of proof

Joanna Landau 2:27 · **ג'ואנה לנדאו** PM

Yes, I agree. But it's a shame to think that just because there are lots of people who think that way, and express themselves online in really horrible ways, that all of us are like that, don't you think?

I've never been to Pakistan, have you been to Israel?

OCT 10

Joanna Landau 8:27 · **ג'ואנה לנדאו** AM

Hi Daud, I hope one day we can visit one another's countries. Until then, from my experience all I can say is that most Israelis don't hate Muslims at all. We have Muslim friends and work colleagues. I'm sad you have a different picture of our people, but can't blame you for it. I hope eventually you'll discover that most of us just want to live in Peace and not hate anyone. Wishing you all the best 🌼

Daud ▉▉▉ 1:16 PM

You are right, not all Israelis hate Muslims but most

Before we go on, we ask you to remember this:

The BDS movement relies on pro-Israel responses like our bodies rely on oxygen, because only if we continue to respond will the social media algorithm keep the conversation alive. If we starve the BDS of our response, thereby *deflating the crisis* rather than amplifying it, we will deplete the movement of its oxygen to keep going. It won't go away altogether, but it will be far less impactful. It is up to us, and requires a tremendous amount of self-control.

THE DAY AFTER

Have you ever considered that Operation Guardian of the Walls lasted for all of *eleven* days, from start to finish? Think about that. Just eleven days.

Are we really going to let eleven days define Israel's image for months and years to come? Since the answer to this question is partially up to us, it should be a resounding *no!*

We — Israel's stakeholders, **not our detractors — decide what Israel's narrative should be.** Yes, there are competing narratives on social media about Israel, and there may be a sense that the negative narrative is prevailing. Yet the truth of the matter is that, due to the nature of the beast, these competing narratives mostly live side by side and *often don't even meet.* Meaning, millions of Next Gen'ers are completely oblivious to the fact that a massive fight is going on online over who's right and who's wrong in the Israeli-Palestinian conflict, as we've shown in previous chapters. *This* is the light at the end of your tunnel, and it shines bright.

For example, there are 80 million Instagram followers who love Gal Gadot, the actor who plays Wonder Woman, and everything she represents — much of which is unabashedly Israeli. At the same time, people also love Bella Hadid, who, as we've already noted, has around 56 million followers on the same platform. The daughter of a Palestinian man who chastises Israel for (he claims) driving his family out of their home during the War of Independence, Hadid tweets often and without mercy against Israel. This should come as no surprise, considering her upbringing and worldview. Yet that conversation on Hadid's feed has not caused Gadot to lose followers. If Hadid were as powerful as we all give her credit for, Gadot's popularity would have faded, fast. As it turns out, during the months following Operation Guardian of the Walls, not only did Gadot not lose followers, but her following actually *increased*![7]

We see the same phenomenon — attraction to Israel's offering despite condemnation of its policies — in a completely different field: Israel's tech industry. As depicted in Figure 8.1, in the past two decades this industry has gone from strength to strength.

Surely, if so many people consider Israel to be a pariah state, wouldn't it be hard for us to be one of the world's strongest innovation-based economies? Especially considering our economy is export-based and therefore reliant on bilateral trade relations with many countries?

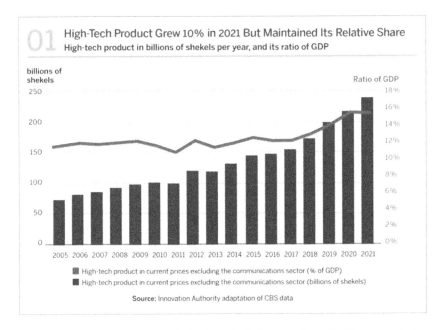

Figure 8.1. Growth of Israel's high-tech industry since 2005, around the same time the BDS movement was launched at the World Economic Forum summit in Davos, Switzerland.

Here's the bottom line: is there a negative narrative against Israel out there? Yes, there is. But a very positive narrative also exists by its side, far less harmed than you have been led to believe by even the worst media-related crises that afflict Israel. And those millions and millions of people who *do* want to connect with Israel are still out there for the taking — before and, especially, after the crisis.

Consequently, once the immediate, on-the-ground crisis (i.e., the war itself) is over, we recommend that you *double down* on positive messaging about Israel, in line with everything else we have already shared with you in this book. **Use the other Ethical Tribing tactics to shine a light and boost positive awareness for Israel, so that it drowns out the negative narrative promulgated during the crisis, as much as possible.**

CONNECTING THE DOTS

At some point, sadly, there *will* be another flare-up on social media relating to Israel. It's inevitable. We suggest that the next time it happens, try to be *smart* about how to manage it, even though you'd rather be *right*. It's hard, but doable. And if you keep your eye on the ultimate objective — which is that millions of young people view Israel positively and want to connect with it — it is not only doable; it is an imperative.

• Because of a variety of external realities that we have little to no control over, it is extremely difficult to change people's minds about anything on social media, not least about Israel in relation to the conflict. As a result, social media is the least effective platform on which to be successful in traditional Israel Advocacy. In other words, we're fighting a losing battle. If you accept this axiom, now you can think of more productive ways to handle the next crisis online.

• A great reputation isn't measured just by when times are good. It's an especially important foundation to have for when times are bad. That's why, the day after the crisis is over, we must double down on the positive promotion of Israel, building trust and loyalty among the Next Gen toward Israel *before* the next crisis descends upon us.

• And when the situation goes bad again, implement the following tactics: (1) Don't engage publicly, because that wakes up the algorithm which leads to more awareness of Israel in negative contexts; but (2) Do engage privately, through the chat function, where you have time to develop rapport and a real conversation with the other person; and in so doing, (3) Use persuasion and influence methodologies to manage your response.

———————

We've got one more tactic left to complete the Ethical Tribing strategy. We thank you for reaching this point and hope that you're starting to see the light in what often feels like a desperate situation.

In the final chapter of Part II, we will talk about the importance of *tracking* how people feel about Israel using data, and *tweaking* Israel-related messaging and digital efforts for maximum impact. Both are needed in order to decide where we go from here.

9 | Tactic 6: Track and Tweak

"Marketing without data is like driving with your eyes closed."

— Dan Zarrella

When the events of 9/11 happened, Israeli civil servant Ido Aharoni, whom we referred to earlier in this book, had just assumed his role as consul for media and public affairs in the United States (a decade later, he was appointed consul general for Israel in New York). In a recent article he wrote where he was looking back at this watershed global event from the perspective of how it could have affected Israel, Aharoni recalled:

> "It was clear to us all at the consulate that this was an event of biblical proportions."[1]

At the time when the 9/11 attacks took place, the consulate had just retained the services of a public relations magnate, the late Howard Rubenstein, who was brought in quickly to advise them how to react.

"Keep quiet," Rubenstein said. "This is not your event. Stay out of it."

"It was very smart advice. Too bad few Israeli officials listened to Rubenstein," Aharoni quipped in his recollection of the ensuing months and years.

The overzealous reaction by the government and Jewish community to the event — insisting that Israel had a much bigger role to play in the unfolding story than it really did — led Aharoni to want to dig deeper. He wanted to examine the research and carefully glean how Americans truly felt about Israel at the time:

> "Through a series of studies conducted by the Brand Israel Group, a team of experts that volunteered to provide insight to Israel's diplomats in the US, we discovered that the situation is more complicated than we thought: Sadly, Israel was better known than liked."

The studies Aharoni was referring to included what eventually became known as the "House Exercise": an extensive qualitative study made up of ten focus groups that were conducted across the United States in 2005, with participants aged eighteen to seventy-four who thought they were being invited to a discussion about "America and the world." They didn't know it was specific to Israel.

Each group was instructed to imagine they were in a town somewhere in the United States. All along Main Street there were houses, with each house representing a country. To kick off the exercise, participants were asked to provide a list of countries, off the top of their head, that they would wish to visit. The purpose of this question was to ascertain whether Israel was a "top-of-mind" country (the first brand that comes to mind when thinking about a specific category) — as its stakeholders clearly thought it was. Unsurprisingly, in not one of the focus groups did "Israel" come up unaided.

In other words, contrary to what the Israeli government and the Jewish community thought at the time — and probably still thinks — Israel is not such a hot topic for Americans.

With "Israel" inserted nonetheless into the list of houses, participants were to "go into" each house and describe what it looked like, who was living there, and how it felt while they were inside. Off they went, each group to a different house per the list they had compiled. Around the fourth or fifth house, before they started getting tired, they entered the Israeli house.

The following is a verbatim account of reactions by participants, taken from the recording of the groups from behind a two-way mirror, as is standard in qualitative studies. To protect the participants' identities, these videos cannot be found online:

"Is there a lawn?" asked a moderator about the Israeli house. "Mmmm, no," answered the group. One group said that "there's a lot of concrete" and that "it's not very attractive." A moderator of another group asked if there was anything colorful about the exterior of the house, and all of the participants, almost in unison, answered, "No!"

Sadly, it went downhill from there, with all groups, regardless of age, gender, political leaning, or socioeconomic status. You see, contrary to what they imagined an Italian house looked and felt like (lots of children, everyone eating spaghetti, playing cards, and drinking *vino*, a house they would be glad to spend all day in), these Americans weren't describing a house at all when it comes to Israel.

In their minds, "Israel" was likened to a one-story bunker, with bars on the windows and barbed wire surrounding it, keeping people out. The father — a religious man — greets the group at the door. The house is kosher, the vibe is "strict, serious, uncomfortable." Only about four people live in the Israeli house (compared with a full Italian house). Some of the participants weren't sure they would be welcome because of religious restrictions. An African American man in one group said he was "not sure they'll accept me because of my skin color."

When it was time to go, they didn't need to be prompted, like in the Italian house; they *wanted* to leave. Some could be heard saying "glad we're out of there" and "hope we get out safe." They talked about Israel in terms of what they saw on TV — that it was "dangerous, just because of all that's going on over there."

At some point the moderator challenged them: "Let's say there's a neighborhood block party. Would all the families go, do you think?" One of the participants in a group of women in their thirties responded, "I don't think the Israeli[ans] would go." Another woman disagreed: "I think the father would go, just to see," and yet another added, "But I don't think he'd allow the children to go, or maybe not even the wife."

"I just get the feeling that they're very defensive and protective," an older woman in another group said. And another man, in yet another group, opined that "they are people that would just like to be left alone, with animosity towards others." No less tellingly, a man in his fifties said, "I don't know what more to expect from Israel's house than I do from France's or India's."

Ultimately, the conclusion from the study was that when Americans think of Israel, they think of "conflict" and "religion," and that they are totally turned off by the country (even if they agreed with its policies relating to the conflict — which most of them did).

———————

We are not sharing this story to depress you. We recount it here because we think it's a massive wake-up call for anyone interested in Israel's global image. It sowed the seeds — that took far too long to sprout — of the Israeli government and Jewish community's understanding that the lens through which they were telling Israel's story had to be broadened if they wanted Israel to thrive, not just survive.

Only an observant few paid attention at first, but the data was there and allowed them to believe wholeheartedly in an approach that was very different from the mainstream thinking at the time among the pro-Israel community.

That's the power of robust data — it not only helps you to see the light, but it also gives you the confidence to keep on walking in that light's direction.

TRACK

According to a 2022 Statista report,[2] the global revenue of the market research industry exceeded $76.4 billion in 2021, growing more than twofold since 2008. Obviously, if market research weren't needed, it wouldn't be such a hot, multibillion-dollar industry. So we can all agree that being data-driven is essential to growth and success.

To this end, large sums of money are indeed invested by the Israeli government, and by the Jewish community in the Diaspora, on research about Israel. One type of study focuses on Jewish people's feelings toward their own Jewish identity, their attitudes toward Israel, and their experiences with anti-Semitism. Another set of studies centers on what people globally (Jewish and non-Jewish) think of Israel in connection with the conflict.

These latter studies always ask the same question, along the lines of: "Thinking about the Israeli-Palestinian conflict, are you more sympathetic to the Israelis or the Palestinians?" Whenever a new poll about Israel by the Pew Research Center, Gallup, or YouGov is published, Israeli and Jewish media is filled with its findings. Even more so when these polls are conducted by Jewish organizations. We have referred to several of both kinds of studies throughout this book.

Unfortunately, a significantly smaller amount of money and attention is directed at the kind of research that *other countries do all the time* to find out what global citizens are thinking about them on a range of features. These countries then devise national branding and marketing strategies based on the information they have collected. One example is Brand USA,[3] which consistently tracks[4] how people feel about America for the purposes of travel. Another is New Zealand Story, which tracks global perceptions toward the country's business and travel offerings.[5]

We should note that there *are* a handful of organizations that do this kind of research for Israel, and certainly the Israeli government invests in research and data collection, but the findings aren't always shared with the rest of the community or conducted often enough.

This kind of data collection is very different from the others studies we mentioned above, and usually includes:

1. A review of global surveys such as the Best Countries Index, the Global Soft Power Index, and the Nation Brands Index, as well as other annual publications on *perceptions* toward countries.

2. Research on country-specific perceptions commissioned from agencies that specialize in place branding and marketing (you can access Vibe Israel's top-level reports of its research about Israel since 2018 on our website[6]).

3. Owned and earned media analytics from the social media platforms of government ministries and NGOs that provide deep insights into how well people are engaging with these accounts, how long they stay on their websites, which posts are more viral than others, etc.

4. Sentiment tracking and analysis when doing digital campaigns, to ascertain reactions to them, with social listening software offered by companies such as Talkwalker, Buzzilla, and the like.

5. Qualitative data such as in-depth interviews and focus groups like the ones conducted about Israel in 2005.

To get a snapshot of Israel's global image at any given time, *all* of the above forms of data collection need to be

undertaken periodically, not just the kind that is focused on what people think of Israel in connection with the conflict. Why? Because if we're in the business of marketing and branding Israel, and not just Advocating for it, then what we need to know is how members of the Next Gen *feel* about Israel, and not just what they *think*.

The bottom line is this: data should be driving your strategy and tactics right from the start.

So, if you plan to invest in promoting Israel to a specific audience, start with doing a situational analysis of how that audience currently feels toward Israel. Find the gaps between what they perceive Israel to be, and what Israel truly is, so that you know how to fill them. Data should then accompany you throughout the process: from researching what kind of messaging — on or offline — is working right now, through tracking the success of the campaign you choose to go for, all the way up to evaluating its impact once it's over.

Which leads us to the importance of tracking for *performance evaluation purposes* and *improvement*. The reason you track is not only to help guide you in your current efforts; you also track to learn what can be tweaked and improved upon *in future campaigns*.

TWEAK

Malcolm Gladwell, the prolific author and public speaker, in his first and most famous book, *The Tipping Point*,[7] talks about the "Stickiness Factor" and compares a viral epidemic to a word-of-mouth epidemic. In both cases, he claims, it is the messenger that matters, for they are the vehicle through which a message (or virus) spreads. We shared a similar sentiment in the "Messenger Is the Message" section of the "Strategic Storytelling" chapter.

> "But the content of the message matters too," Gladwell writes. "And the specific quality that a message needs to be successful is the quality of 'stickiness.' Is the message . . . memorable? Is it so memorable, in fact, that it can create change, that it can spur someone to action?"[8]

Gladwell is not very specific about how this Stickiness Factor is obtained, and he suggests that the stickiness of a message can often be determined only *by testing and experimentation*. In many of the examples that he provides in the relevant chapter of his book,[9] he shows how the initial packaging of a message is often not the stickiest one, and it is only when the message is repackaged and tweaked several times that the Stickiness Factor kicks in and the message goes viral. We — and pretty much any marketer with experience — agree with Gladwell's conclusion. We believe that resting on laurels, even if a campaign is doing well, is never the right way to consistently do better.

It would be advisable, for these purposes, to take a page out of an army book: after every operation — small or large — an army conducts an After Action Review (AAR) to uncover what worked and what didn't. The objective is not to call out those who failed, but rather to learn from failures in order to improve execution next time.

This thinking can and should be applied to our "battle" for hearts and minds for Israel. If, after every Israel-related event, or social media campaign or mission, you conduct an AAR and really drill down into what worked and what didn't, then you'll know how to repackage and tweak the things that didn't go as well as they could, so that next time they will. A DAR, or During Action Review, may even be in order, to tweak on-the-go (for example, with paid promotion).

As an example, at the end of every Vibe Tour, the tour manager sits with the influencers and asks them for feedback, especially the not-so-good reviews. The organization wants to hear them, so we can do better next time.

Read on for a case study that pulls together all the pieces of the Track and Tweak tactic, with profound results.

CASE STUDY: DIGITAL CAMPUS CAMPAIGNS

Earlier in the book, we referenced a digital project that Vibe Israel did in 2022 to gauge perceptions about Israel held by college students in three cities (Atlanta, Miami, and San Francisco), and shift them in Israel's favor. Here's how it came to be, and how we used data tracking and tweaking to enhance its impact:

1. It began with a conversation we had with a friend of Michael's: a major Jewish philanthropist in America who has supported pro-Israel and Holocaust-related causes for decades. He immediately agreed with our point of view about Israel's less than optimal PR strategy and what our community should be doing instead. This man is not young, but his sharp mind and business savvy prompted him to ask us the following questions:

"How do you prove this actually works? That all the great stuff these influencers share on social media actually changes or shapes opinions about Israel? Can you get evidence that shows that these Next Gen'ers can shift from feeling indifferent to feeling positive?"

He concluded:

"I believe if you can prove that by running a pilot program that gets you hard data, then the community will back a project to scale it."

2. Vibe already did pre- and post-surveys on its tour participants and used social listening software to track the reach, engagement levels, and sentiment of the content generated by every tour. But some of these numbers were falling on deaf ears, because they were so complicated and also because donors were looking for exactly what Michael's friend had highlighted: a *shift in opinion* about Israel, not just a warm and fuzzy reaction to great digital content about it. So we accepted the challenge.

3. Because Vibe Tours were not operating at that time due to COVID-19 restrictions, we were unable to conduct a survey on the followers of Vibe Tours influencers to see if what these influencers posted was indeed shifting followers' perceptions of Israel. So we decided to deploy a digital campaign using positive content about Israel from video material that Vibe had collected from past tours over the years, and to target a specific demographic that was of interest to the community.

4. To spearhead the project, Michael brought on Hauswirth/ Co, a leading Chicago-based digital media consultancy he had worked with on cause-oriented campaigns. Our research homed in on demographic groups that many in

the community have been curious to learn more about: progressive Black Americans and US Latine college students. A survey by YouGov indicated that among adults thirty and under, a far higher proportion of Black and Latine respondents were "more likely to believe anti-Semitic stereotypes than white respondents."[10] If this data was accurate, did it also reflect the attitudes of these groups on college campuses? We wanted to find out.

5. To understand how this demographic currently views Israel, in order to figure out what messaging might have the best impact on them, we began with a survey that focused on their general perceptions of Israel.

6. To get a snapshot of what specific areas of Israel's offering we wanted to concentrate on promoting, we reviewed Pew Research Center data and other reports about the political views of these particular Gen Z'ers toward Israel, then Vibe's own global research findings, and also the latest data about Israel in the Global Soft Power and the Best Countries indices. For example, Israel performs quite poorly under the "fun" attribute presented in the external perception studies (as can be seen on pages 194 and 195 below), so we knew we wanted the campaign to project a very colorful, vibrant, and fun aspect of Israel.

7. Hauswirth/Co and Vibe partnered with market insights leader Qualtrics, which works with nearly 90 percent of Fortune 100 companies. The firm surveyed a sample of 900 people, 300 from each city. The results, some of which we have already mentioned, ranged from obvious to shocking:

   • Overall, the first words they associated with Israel were "Religion" and "Jewish" (77 percent), and at a distant second was "Violence and warfare" (11 percent).

"Innovation and technology" came in at a meager 6.1 percent (*Start-Up Nation*, anyone?), then "Sun and beaches" with just 3 percent, and, finally, 4 percent said "Don't know" or "Nothing."

- Most of these Gen Z'ers (80 percent) reported hearing about Israel on the news or social media, and yet when asked what their general perception of Israel was, *50 percent reported having a favorable opinion, and 40 percent had no opinion at all.* Just 9 percent reported a negative opinion about Israel.

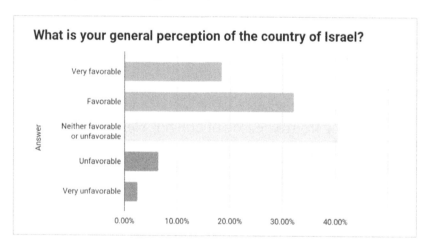

Figure 9.1. Slide from the Hauswirth/Co report *Digital Campus Campaigns.*[11]

- A majority of respondents said they would buy Israeli products or services (76 percent) or consider traveling to Israel for a vacation (67 percent). According to Kevin Hauswirth, Hauswirth/Co's principal, this is an indicator of brand preference. So, if an Israeli product, service, or travel opportunity were presented to these Next Gen'ers in the Supermarket of Nations, they said they were amenable to choosing it over competing "products."

8. Beyond the answers we received about respondents' first associations with Israel, we were extremely encouraged to hear how positive the rest of the responses were. We actually asked ourselves: was this too good to be true? In the face of so much of the negative news and anecdotal feedback that we hear regularly, the data surprised us. **But that's the whole point of *trusting in the data.*** And now that we were armed with the knowledge that Gen Z'ers *were* in fact open to positive messaging about Israel, we set out to further scrutinize these results by deploying a narrow and focused digital campaign to test the findings.

9. To decide which content would work best for the campaign, we tapped into Vibe's knowledge and experience stemming from a decade of bringing Next Gen digital influencers to Israel. We chose three Passion Points that had worked well on Vibe Tours and had continued to trend well in 2022: Wellness, Travel, and Pets. We shared our social media listening reports from past tours with Hauswirth/Co, which showed which of the social media posts were most viral and engaging, and Hauswirth's content creators developed a series of thirty-second bilingual video ads to promote on Facebook and Instagram. The ads were branded very prominently as being associated with Israel. Our intention was to go "loud and proud." We did not hide the fact that we were confident we had something great to share about Israel.

10. During the three weeks we invested in ad promotion on Facebook and Instagram, the Hauswirth/Co team optimized the campaign to get the maximum number

of people in our target audience to see our ads. With an investment of $30,000, we achieved 6.9 million ad impressions to this specific audience. Ad impressions are defined as the number of times the ads appeared in total. We reached 168,612 people across the three markets who clicked 4,659 times in response to the ad's call-to-action message: "Want to know more? Click here." After clicking the ad, the target audience was led to Vibe Israel's digital toolbox of professional photos and videos of Israel that are geared toward a young demographic.

11. On average, users saw the ad 4.6 times and stopped to play the videos 3.5 million times. There were only three negative comments during the entire three weeks.

12. We then repeated the survey, using an industry standard "Ad Recall" filter question ("Do you recall seeing this ad on your feed recently?"), to get a second round of responses from the same demographic. We did this so we could compare them with the first round and see the change. The ad was clearly "sticky," as indicated by an Ad Recall rate 3.5 times the industry average on Facebook.

13. The findings were conclusive: exposure to a targeted brand campaign dramatically shifted the perceptions of these college students. In just three weeks:

- Those already favorable (32 percent "favorable" and 18 percent "very favorable" in the first study) reported higher levels of favorability (36 percent "favorable" and 40 percent "very favorable"). This meant that *a full half of the 40 percent* who were "neither favorable nor unfavorable" shifted into the favorable section. No less importantly, the number of people who said they were "unfavorable" and "very unfavorable" was *slashed in half*. Those stats moved from 6 percent "unfavorable" to 3 percent, and from 2.5 percent "very unfavorable" to 1 percent.

- No longer surprised, we were also heartened to see an increase of 13 percent in the number of respondents who said they would buy Israeli products or services, and a decrease of just over 40 percent in those who said they wouldn't. Similarly, the percentage of those who said they would consider traveling to Israel increased from 67 percent to 89 percent, and the share of those who said they wouldn't decreased from 33 percent to 11 percent.

- Finally, going back to the first association this demographic had for Israel, "Religion" and "Jewish" were still the front-runners, but 8 percent less; "Innovation and technology" increased from 6 percent to 11 percent; "Violence and warfare" decreased from 11 percent to 9 percent; "Sun and beaches" doubled from 2.5 percent to 5 percent; and "Don't know / Nothing" increased from 4 percent to 5 percent.

14. In addition to having clear indicators that the campaign worked, and that we were able to meet the philanthropist's challenge, we gathered valuable information for future reference, such as: in which of the three cities the campaign was most successful; which of the specific audiences within the demographics we chose was most engaged; and which content worked best. All of this is information that can be used to make *future campaigns even more successful.*

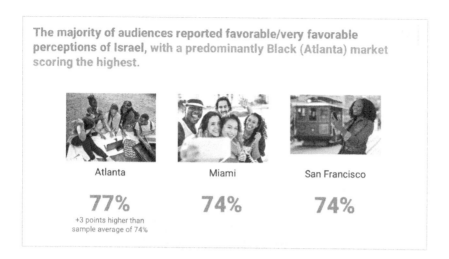

Figure 9.2. Slide from the Hauswirth/Co report *Digital Campus Campaigns.*[12]

We present this case to you to demonstrate just how important data collection, tracking, and tweaking are to the success of a campaign. Could we have proceeded without all the data collection, analysis, and repackaging? Absolutely. But then we would have been — as the quote that opened this chapter says — *driving with our eyes closed*. We may not have crashed, but we certainly wouldn't have reached the checkered flag so quickly and effectively.

The Best Countries Index – a country ranking published annually in U.S. News & World Report, in partnership with the Wharton School of Business and WPP's BrandAsset Valuator®, ranked Israel in thirtieth place out of eighty-five in 2022. Approximately twenty thousand people are surveyed for this ranking, split evenly between informed elites, business decision-makers, and the general public (over the age of eighteen).

A deeper dive into the methodology, subcategories, and responses reveals a lot of important information about how people perceive Israel. For example, what drives Israel up in the overall ranking is its perceived strength in the Power category ("a leader, economically influential, strong exports, politically influential, strong international alliances, strong military"). While on the face of it, Israel ranking high here is a good thing, these qualities and strengths resonate far less with the Next Gen than older generations. By contrast, under the Adventure category ("friendly, fun, good for tourism, pleasant climate, scenic, sexy"), Israel ranks extremely poorly, in 74th place. Yet, if you know Israel, you know that in reality, it ranks very highly in all of the attributes of the Adventure category.

These gaps can be exposed only through data gathering that is empiric.

https://www.usnews.com/news/best-countries/articles/methodology

https://www.usnews.com/news/best-countries/israel

CONNECTING THE DOTS

Ethical Tribing does not operate in an emotionally driven vacuum. Rather, it is a data-driven strategy that takes full advantage of 21st century snapshot technology to know how to steer efforts in the most productive direction. The guessing games are over.

• By conducting research about Israel, any strategy developed will rest on reality and not on idyllic or paranoid notions of what we *assume* people think and feel about Israel. This is absolutely essential to the success of our communal mission. Pew, Gallup, and other polls tend to focus on political perceptions, but they paint only part of the picture. The community should invest in a wide variety of other sources to know how the Next Gen *feels* toward Israel.

• By evaluating the real-time sentiments and reactions to Israel-related digital content that is being distributed, you can ensure that — after some modification, tweaking, and repackaging — your messaging sticks, and that you get the biggest bang for your buck.

In the digital era, it is incumbent upon us as a community to leverage the gift of technology to benefit Israel and the Jewish People. But this kind of activity must be data-driven and supported by industry-standard market research, solid advice by digital marketing and branding professionals, and a good deal of common sense.

We have come to the end of Part II, in which we laid out the six R.E.S.P.C.T. tactics of our strategy. We hope that by now you, too, recognize that thanks to the unprecedented speed and reach of the digital realm, the stars are lining up *right now* for Ethical Tribing to have a profound impact on young adults when it comes to Israel and the future of Jewish Peoplehood.

Conclusion:
We Are All Nachshon

"I never did anything alone. Whatever was accomplished in this country was accomplished collectively."

— Golda Meir

In the first sentence of this book, we told you that our motivation in writing *Ethical Tribing* was quite personal. Since you are still with us, we can safely assume that it is personally important to you too. For your enthusiasm, we are profoundly grateful.

In the Introduction, we presented our best fact-based case to make clear that in recent years, the Jewish community has witnessed the beginning of a worrying trend: a smaller proportion of the Next Generation identifying as Jewish and/or feeling connected to Israel (whether they are Jewish or not).

We explained how this growing gap could develop into a serious long-term threat to our people. If the trend continues, it is almost certain to result in two dire consequences. The first is a Jewish Tribe that is smaller and weaker. The second is a new generation of public voices and decision-makers — Jewish and non-Jewish — who have no affinity for Israel and, therefore, no incentive to understand and respect it for the special country that it is.

Without intervention, it is only a matter of time.

We fully understand how uncomfortable it can be to read and consider these ominous prospects. But the gravity of our people's predicament is precisely why we need to spell it out as straightforwardly as possible. These are hard truths to face. For all of us. Yet telling the hard truths is one of the purest forms of love.

All of us who have this love for Israel want our country and the Jewish People to stand tall and flourish as long as planet Earth keeps turning. At the same time, we know full well that simply wanting it isn't enough; *we have to make it happen.*

This is why we wrote *Ethical Tribing* — because we wanted to offer a blueprint for how to turn collective aspirations into on-the-ground reality.

RECAP: NEW PARADIGMS

We've given you a lot to digest over the past ten chapters, so it's time to do a final review. In Part I of *Ethical Tribing*, we laid out the paradigm shifts in thinking that are required to start telling Israel's story in a way that will engage the Next Generation.

We started by defining the "Social (Life) Media Revolution," which is far more than a destination or activity for young people today. Social media is where their virtual lives interact and overlap with almost everything that they do offline. For Israel, it represents a massive opportunity — which is currently only scratching the surface of its potential — to engage the Next Gen on *their terms*.

In "The Supermarket of Nations," we explained why no country can afford to sit on the sidelines and not make an effort to compete for talent, tourism, trade dollars, and national reputation. Israel, as much as or more than any other country, must be in the game and project its unique competitive advantages in order to stand out. We need to go after every Next Gen shopper who's in the market for a new place to explore.

The third and final shift in thinking that we introduced was "The Engagement Ladder," a venerated marketing model that we contoured specifically for Ethical Tribing. It begins with an effort to grab the audience's *Attention*, and then to ensure that they are *Attracted* to what they're seeing. When the content that we're presenting to them about Israel is genuinely interesting and inspiring, they will become more likely to take *Action*. And once that action has delivered real value, we hope they will climb up the final step of The Engagement Ladder to become *Advocates* — helping Israel by getting their peers to start climbing it too.

RECAP: R.E.S.P.C.T.

In Part II of the book, we presented the six tactics of the Ethical Tribing strategy that can be used to motivate young people to start scaling The Engagement Ladder. We vigorously argued the case — and hopefully proved to you — that when we implement all of these elements at once, ethically and with intention, we will maximize the impact that we're trying to make in our outreach efforts to the Next Gen:

- **Radical Empathy:** Putting ourselves in the Next Gen's shoes and seeing the world through their eyes.
- **Emotional Hook:** Learning about what our audience loves, what their Passion Points are — and tailoring new, Israel-infused content to them.
- **Strategic Storytelling:** Sharing a professionally crafted Israel Story with intention and through compelling messengers.
- **Pay-to-Play:** Engaging indifferent audiences by investing in paid promotion (on a grand scale), because there's no other way to reach them today.
- **Crisis Deflation:** When controversy flares up, using restraint online so as not to fan the flames.
- **Track and Tweak:** Applying data to maximize both audience reach and messaging impact.

The R.E.S.P.C.T. tactics are grounded in the sciences of influence and persuasion, and they leverage the power of social media to connect with the audience that Israel most needs to engage. Used ethically, they comprise the foundational components needed to see the change we all hope for.

ALL UPSIDE

One of Ethical Tribing's greatest strengths as a strategy is that it is **risk-free**. There's no downside. Because it is based on the targeted sharing of positive, interesting, relevant, and authentic content about Israel, it is not controversial. It cannot be argued away, or dismissed as a fabricated portrayal of the Israeli people by our detractors, if the audience is *genuinely* drawn to it. If the messenger and message are authentic, true reflections of the reality on the ground, Israel's story will take hold.

We have seen this in action already: from the success of the Israeli tech sector to Gal Gadot's fame and appeal, to the popularity of the city of Tel Aviv among progressive, adventurous Next Gen'ers. Doubling down on more of this kind of positive content appearing on the social media feeds of young people can only lead to one result: more of them connecting positively with Israel. So the community has nothing to lose — and *everything to gain*.

This is especially the case when it comes to our own Tribe. The Israeli people have a truly amazing spirit, history, and culture that the Jewish People should always be able to take great pride in. Every single person who feels this way ought to be able to express their pride in what our people have achieved and continue to break new ground on every day — without even a hint of hesitation. Sadly, this is not the case right now. Earlier, we cited two statistics from an AJC survey about the roughly 25 percent of millennial Jews who've said that negative perceptions of Israel have damaged their friendships — and that they have distanced themselves from Israel to better fit in with their social circles.[1]

Ethical Tribing is designed to turn those trends on their heads. By proactively sharing Israel's story with the Next Gen — telling it in a way that aligns with their values and interests — Israel will be able to attract new supporters in a totally positive fashion. And we know that through the power of Social

Proofing, the new feelings that are generated about Israel will become contagious. There's a reason people use the expression "going viral."

We recognize that we are not inventing the wheel here. Several of the tactics we've outlined in R.E.S.P.C.T. have been practiced before. But not *en masse,* and not all together as part of an overarching strategy. To achieve the kind of scale with the Next Gen that will make a meaningful difference, everyone who loves Israel is invited to get in on the action — including the millennials and Gen Z'ers *who are already in the tent!*

Katey Goldman is one of them. A twenty-year-old student at the University of Wisconsin who recently experienced Israel through Birthright, Goldman says she's planning on returning — and bringing new people with her:

> "I think Israel is a place where people my age *do* want to be. And social media allows people to see other people's experiences, realize what they're doing — and how amazing it is."

It's not much more complicated than that.

And just think of the benefits that will accrue once a great many more Jewish Next Gen'ers feel the way that Goldman does. Anyone who has felt anxiety over expressing pride in Israel will not have to negotiate that stress anymore. Collectively, Jews and non-Jews who feel a positive connection with Israel will have less angst, more calm, and less debate. These will be our wins when we have more people thinking positively about Israel.

We are not oblivious to reality, though. We fully recognize that Israel is a complex, imperfect brand. Israel's government may do things the world finds hard to understand and accept, and some vocal pro-Israel supporters may not align with Next Gen values. If history is any guide, and we know that it is, Israel will continually be impelled to engage in defensive military operations that cause some people to fan the flames of anti-Zionism on- and offline. This is part and parcel of Israel's brand; we know this to be true and do not suggest that it can be circumvented with savvy marketing campaigns.

But if the positive outweighs the negative, there will be less strife and more harmony. Instead of feeling as if the gloomy cloud centered on the conflict is constantly following us around, the community will be engaged in far more conversations about the common affinity that a growing number of people have for Israel. Wouldn't that be wonderful?

If striving for the halcyon atmosphere we've just described sounds a bit quixotic, we understand. Finding transformational solutions to any kind of persistent and seemingly intractable problem can feel like a pretty tall order. But the reason that we feel so comfortable in predicting this kind of future for Israel is that we have *seen it work before.* We've shared stories with you about other countries where rebranding strategies have changed entire trajectories. There are precedents for Ethical Tribing.

Bearing all of this in mind, doesn't it make sense for those of us who care deeply for Israel to give this approach a full shot? If the old game plan hasn't reaped the changes in perceptions of Israel that the community seeks, and if there is nothing to lose by calling some new plays, isn't it incumbent on all of us to do so? Shouldn't we join forces, hit the field, and work as one to strengthen the future of Israel and the Jewish People?

We hope you agree that the easy answer to these questions is: **Yalla! Let's go!**

STRENGTH IN NUMBERS

The last person we're going to quote in this book is a legendary rabbinical figure who lived in 18th Lithuania. Rabbi Schneur Zalman of Liady was the founder of Chabad, an influential form of Hasidic Judaism that places great emphasis on the value of wisdom, understanding and knowledge. He was also a prolific writer. In a collection of his teachings that were first published in 1796, Rabbi Zalman wrote the following:

> "The people of Israel compose a single soul. Only the bodies are separate."

When we first came across this expression, we were instantly struck by its graceful simplicity. It also hit an obvious thematic chord with us: the rabbi beautifully described how he viewed the unity of our Tribe. And his words feel timeless.

But the other reason that we share Rabbi Zalman's thought here is what he wrote in his second sentence. Though he was speaking philosophically, the reality is that the actual "bodies" that make up our people *do* matter a great deal. Especially today. The actions that each one of us takes as an individual — or does not take — have consequences.

One hundred and fifty-two years after Rabbi Zalman wrote those wise words, the Jewish People established the modern

State of Israel. Think of the extraordinary successes that have been accomplished — just in the past seventy-five years! Not one scintilla of it happened accidentally or easily. We owe a debt of gratitude to so many who have sacrificed so much.

And now it's *our* generation's turn.

We hope you will join us in this movement to connect the Next Generation to Israel in the digital era — in whatever fashion suits you best. In that spirit, we've included a menu of options below to help you get involved.

And while we candidly asserted in the "Pay-to-Play" chapter that there is an urgent need for major financial investment to optimally reach and influence our intended audience, the fact is that most movements don't happen in a heartbeat. So very often, it is the humble foot soldiers who valiantly push for what they believe in day-to-day that ultimately lead to a movement's breakthrough inflection point.

The Ethical Tribing strategy is a game of not only addition, but multiplication. The ripple effect. *We do this together*. No one is excluded. Here are some of the ways to participate in this cause, depending on your own individual involvement in the field:

Philanthropists

- Lead the way or bring together a consortium of donors to reignite and update the process that Vibe Israel started in 2018 to rebrand Israel to the Next Gen, and take it to the next level. That process included a five-year work plan, developed in partnership with Bloom Consulting, and included over twenty projects for immediate implementation. It is there for the taking.

- If there are specific types of activities or platforms you feel work best to share Israel's story with the world, *increase* your investment in them. Such activities may include investing in bringing global events to Israel or sponsoring Israelis to appear on global stages; deploying local or national social media campaigns; supporting bringing more influencers — digital or otherwise — to Israel.

- Pick a Passion Point you connect with (e.g., food, social entrepreneurship, health, sustainability) and invest in a long-term strategic plan to rebrand Israel through that specific global area of interest. Joanna can help guide you through this process.

- If you're already involved in an organization that creates content highlighting Israel's appealing offerings, consider supporting it financially to promote that content further with paid ads, brand partnerships, content marketing services, etc.

- To support the entire community, invest in research — local and global — that is not just relating to the Israeli-Palestinian conflict, anti-Semitism, or Jewish identity, but rather to broader Next Gen *perceptions* of Israel.

Professional and Community Organizations

- Let's talk about Ethical Tribing! Plan an event that brings together organizations that are involved in promoting Israel to discuss the topics of this book; invite Joanna and/ or Michael to speak at such an event or on a podcast about Israel's global image or how to fight anti-Semitism and the anti-Zionist movement.

- Increase your social media budgets to promote Israel through a positive lens, and bring on specialists who can support you in the development and deployment of campaigns, brand partnerships with local media platforms, and brand ambassadorships by digital influencers. If you're seeking professionally curated, plug-and-play content, use the free digital assets offered on Vibe Israel's toolbox.[2] And please use the narratives we introduced in "Strategic Storytelling" to tell Israel's Story (endorsed by President Rivlin) *so that they stick.*

- Invest in influencer marketing, just like any other brand does these days. There are myriad ways of doing this, including: partnering with Vibe Israel on a digital influencer tour by providing matching funding; inviting micro-influencers from your community on your missions to Israel; featuring digital influencers with name-recognition at your Israel-related events to increase the likelihood of attendance; celebrating digital influencers who have visited Israel by offering them (paid) opportunities to share their experience with your Next Gen.

- Support your community by inviting Joanna and her professional partners to speak on how to manage the negative narrative about Israel online, or how to talk to your teenagers about Israel.

Individuals

- If you belong to a congregation, Jewish community organization, or any other relevant network, spread the word about the Ethical Tribing mission by sharing the book or encouraging your community to invite Joanna and/or Michael to speak about it.

- Seek out positive content about Israel online and share it with your social circles, on- and offline. Vibe Israel's digital toolbox has a list of links to various websites that offer continuously updated content about Israel that the Next Gen will appreciate.

- Consider encouraging a small group of your close friends, who have never been to Israel, to join you on a trip there (a kind of "personal mission" for friends).

- Watch the *Influence Without Authority* e-course[3] created by Joanna and Ariel Halevi, to prepare for the next time there is an Israeli military operation that reaches global awareness on a heightened scale, especially on social media.

At the beginning of our first chapter, we retold the Talmudic tale of Nachshon ben Aminadav: "the man who jumped into the sea." We grant you, citing this story was a pretty melodramatic example of the value of trying something new! But that was our whole point.

Across so many centuries, again and again, we have seen Jewish heroes take brave actions to change the course of history. To change the future for our people. So many of these events have involved great personal risk. The risking of lives. That profound "do or die" moment when there's barely the blink of an eye in which to make enormously consequential decisions.

The prospect of Israel needing to defend itself militarily is always present. Sadly, there is no way for Israelis to ever let their guard down on that front — not in our lifetimes. But on its own, playing that conventional game of defense will not be enough. There is another fight that is always playing out on a separate battlefield — one of *public perception*.

For over fifty years, since the Six Day War, the pro-Israel community and the Israeli government have used a certain set of armor and skills to fight that fight: traditional Israel Advocacy. This is a valiant effort which must continue in full force, for this kind of advocacy works well with certain audiences.

But not all.

Ethical Tribing is a call to set up a *new division* in the battle for the future of Israel and the Jewish People. This division is based on marketing and branding our homeland and its people. This is not one and the same as Advocating for Israel and defending its policies. An army needs *all* of its divisions in order to win, each with its own specialty and budget, just like any large corporation needs a strong marketing department working on a parallel but separate track to complement a well-funded crisis management department.

As we've mentioned, Ethical Tribing and traditional Israel Advocacy are the furthest things from being mutually exclusive missions; each effort strengthens the other. One more multiplier.

THE LEAP

We would like to conclude by reiterating the long-range challenge that the Jewish People face as we approach the second quarter of the 21st century: an incoming generation that is less connected to Israel than perhaps at any time over the past seventy-five years.

The strength of any tribe is predicated on many factors. One of them is fortitude. Our Tribe most certainly has that base covered. The Jewish People carry forward an almost indescribable heritage of survival.

But another factor that is sure to define the Jewish Tribe in the decades to come is the very size of our own membership. To ignore or deny this fact would be taking the *real* risk. Yet in some of our own quarters, despite recognizing the writing that's already on the wall, the sense of urgency has not yet translated into action.

We cannot stress enough that the time to act is NOW. Our Tribe simply cannot afford to let that trend continue — and we believe Ethical Tribing can ensure that it does not. The full power of the Social (Life) Media Revolution must be harnessed to share Israel's authentically unique story, energy, and competitive advantages to every young person who is open to hearing it. The best part? We know from our own research that this is an *enormous* mass of people.

The hour is upon us. The terrain is ripe. And we have a formula that we know is effective when put to scale. All that remains — for those of us who feel that love in our hearts for Israel and the desire to strengthen our Tribe — is to join hands and charge forward.

To take that leap, just like Nachshon.

Acknowledgments

As co-authors, we have each had the most extraordinary experience writing this book together. And we would specifically like to thank the following people for their amazing advising, editing, and design talents. You undoubtedly made us better, every step of the way. In addition, Joanna would like to acknowledge several people who have been instrumental in her personal as well as Vibe Israel's success over the years, on which much of this book is based.

JOINT ACKNOWLEDGMENTS

From the very beginning, we were so fortunate to have a wonderful group of friends and colleagues who so generously gave their time and wisdom to listen, read, review, and advise us. Michael's folks included Andrew Rashkow, Amy Stoken, Alicia Oberman, Judd Malkin, Rick Hirschhaut, Lonnie Nasatir, Kevin Hauswirth, Argelia Martinez, and Marcus Knowles. For Joanna, Richard Bernstein and Becca Hurowitz provided invaluable input.

Nancy Watkins is as tough a copy editor as we have come across — and we have been grateful for both her patience and her intense attention to detail throughout this writing process.

Our designers, Shawn Hazen and Sarit Vardi, made all of our images sing. There is no question in our minds that they made this book more interesting and understandable through their creative contributions.

Our terrific team at Best Seller Publishing made the business end of this process as easy and productive as possible for us. We are grateful to Bob Harpole, Matthew Schnarr, Meghan McDonald, and Rob Kosberg.

JOANNA'S ACKNOWLEDGMENTS

This book is based on a set of ideas that is more than a decade in the making. The enormous amount of learning that I have experienced through the generosity of so many people as we launched and grew Vibe Israel might require a full chapter. But there are a number of people whom I absolutely must directly acknowledge and thank in this space:

Ambassador Ido Aharoni, for opening my eyes to the world of branding and marketing Israel. This epiphany not only became my calling, but also enabled me to choose Israel all over again and understand better why I continue to make that choice every day.

José Filipe Torres and Malcolm Allen, CEO and president of Bloom Consulting, respectively, who are always available to lend their insights from their vast experience advising other countries, cities, and regions, as well as their work with us on Israel's brand, about how to tell my people's story to the world.

David J. Reibstein, the William S. Woodside Professor and Professor of Marketing at the Wharton School of Business, for sharing with me over the years his knowledge and insights about global perceptions of Israel — far beyond what I expected him to.

Ariel Halevi, for partnering with me on creating the "Influence Without Authority" and "How to Talk to Your Teenager About Israel" e-courses.

Vibe Israel USA's Board: Richard Bernstein, Chairman of the board and all-round mensch, for always being so supportive, bolstering my confidence, and imparting invaluable advice; Mark Reisbaum, our board Secretary, for being a Vibe cheerleader since that day he called me to ask for advice on a VIP tour of Israel for Jewish tech leaders from Silicon Valley. We became fast friends immediately and remain so; Alicia Oberman, for introducing me to Michael, for always sharing such grounded and honest advice, and for the many great meals and drinks we have together whenever we have the good fortune to meet and talk about our lives; and Ori Raphael, for contributing his unique point of view from Texas and providing a fresh perspective on how his (our) generation views Israel.

Vibe Israel's past and current board and members of the Amutah: Ruti Arazi, Ariel Halevi, Inbal Dinari, Justine Zwerling, Ori Goore, Orit Vilker, Orit Zahar, Orly Sheffer, Tammy Azulay, and Tsippi Bukshpan, for being such good friends and supporters, both to me personally and to Vibe's mission and vision.

Becca Hurowitz, our voice in North America, for being my partner at Vibe. Knowing that I am not alone at the helm of this ship, which constantly steers in the opposite direction of the current, is a great source of comfort and morale.

The donors who have supported Vibe from the very beginning, and over the years. Their investment in me and my vision is a treasure that I have never taken for granted. They are the true pioneers, the impact investors in the future of the Jewish People. I am deeply grateful for what they have enabled me and my team to achieve over the years, and I share Vibe's accomplishments with each and every one of them.

The hundreds of influencers I have had the pleasure of hosting in Israel over the years. I have learned so much from them, and I am grateful for the posts, articles, videos and pictures they've shared about Israel that have been seen by hundreds of millions of people all over the world. Reading what they wrote and continue to share about Israel makes my heart soar every time.

My friends and family who have always stood by me, through thick and thin, highs and lows, especially my husband and best friend, Edan, without whom none of this would be possible.

My children, Amit, Mia, and Zoe, for being so proud of my achievements and tremendously supportive of my writing this book. And for being the real reason that I wrote it.

My mother, who inspires me every day to celebrate life and always see the silver lining in any situation. And to my grandmother, in many ways my role model for how much women can achieve in this world. Together with my grandfather, she instilled a love for Israel in my mother, who chose to make Israel her home. That love was imparted to my late brother and me, and that is the flame that burns inside me to this day.

My life coach fifteen years ago, Tal Ronen, who was the first to ask me, "Of all the countries in the world, why Israel?," for helping me discover my calling. And my executive coach in more recent years, Sagi Shahar, who provided me with personal, strategic, and leadership guidance, especially when times got tougher during the pandemic.

And finally, over the best part of fifteen years, I have had the pleasure of working with the best and the brightest employees, partners, suppliers, and advisors. I am grateful to every single person who has been a part of my journey and helped make it happen, especially to the incredibly talented team I surrounded myself with. I sincerely hope that I have offered them back at least a measure of what they've so generously granted to me.

I couldn't have done any of this without *all* of you. Thank you from the bottom of my heart.

References

PREFACE

1   Pew Research Center, Jewish Americans in 2020, May 11,
    2021, https://www.pewresearch.org/religion/2021/05/11/
    jewish-americans-in-2020/.

2   Anti-Defamation League, "ADL Audit Finds Antisemitic Incidents
    in United States Reached All-Time High in 2021," news release,
    April 25, 2022, https://www.adl.org/news/press-releases/
    adl-audit-finds-antisemitic-incidents-in-united-states-reached-all-
    time-high-in.

INTRODUCTION

1   Mendy Kaminker, "Nachshon ben Aminadav: The Man Who
    Jumped Into the Sea," Chabad.org, accessed November 15, 2022,
    https://www.chabad.org/library/article_cdo/aid/2199147/jewish/
    Nachshon-ben-Aminadav-The-Man-Who-Jumped-Into-the-Sea.
    htm.

2   Anti-Defamation League, "ADL Audit Finds Antisemitic Incidents
    in United States Reached All-Time High in 2021," news release,
    April 25, 2022, https://www.adl.org/news/press-releases/
    adl-audit-finds-antisemitic-incidents-in-united-states-reached-all-
    time-high-in.

3   Michael Dimock, "Defining Generations: Where Millennials
    End and Generation Z Begins," Pew Research Center, January
    17, 2019, https://www.pewresearch.org/fact-tank/2019/01/17/
    where-millennials-end-and-generation-z-begins/.

4   Statista, "Resident Population of the United States by Sex and
    Age as of July 1, 2021," July 2022, https://www.statista.com/
    statistics/241488/population-of-the-us-by-sex-and-age/.

5   American Jewish Population Project, "United States of America:
    Total Jewish Population," Steinhardt Social Research Institute,
    Brandeis University, accessed September 3, 2022, https://ajpp.
    brandeis.edu/map.

6   Pew Research Center, *Jewish Americans in 2020*, May 11,
    2021, https://www.pewresearch.org/religion/2021/05/11/
    jewish-americans-in-2020/.

7   American Jewish Congress, "AJC's Survey of American
    Jewish Millennials," 2022, https://www.ajc.org/
    Jewish-Millennial-Survey-2022/American-Jewish-Millennials.

8   Eric Adelstein (partner, AL Media), email message to Michael
    Golden, August 24, 2022.

9   Pew Research Center, "Most Americans Have Not Heard Much or
    Anything About the BDS Movement," May 23, 2022, https://www.
    pewresearch.org/religion/2022/05/26/modest-warming-in-u-s-
    views-on-israel-and-palestinians/05-26-22_israel-report_0-10/.

10 Lydia Saad, "Americans Still Pro-Israel, Though Palestinians
    Gain Support," Gallup, March 17, 2022, https://news.gallup.com/
    poll/390737/americans-pro-israel-though-palestinians-gain-
    support.aspx.

11 Avigail Schneiman, "Navigating Gen Z Israel Conversations,"
    eJewish Philanthropy, August 3, 2022, https://
    ejewishphilanthropy.com/navigating-gen-z-israel-conversations/.

12 Graham Wright, Shahar Hecht, and Leonard Saxe, *Jewish Futures
    Project – Birthright Israel's First Decade of Applicants: A Look*

at the Long-term Program Impact, Brandeis University Cohen Center for Modern Jewish Studies, November 2020, https://bir.brandeis.edu/bitstream/handle/10192/39072/jewish-futures-wave6-110620.pdf.

13 Momentum Unlimited, *Looking Back, Dreaming Forward: 2019 Impact Report*, 2020, https://momentumunlimited.org/wp-content/uploads/2020/06/AR_2019_WEB.pdf.

14 American Jewish Congress, "AJC's Survey of American Jewish Millennials," 2022, https://www.ajc.org/Jewish-Millennial-Survey-2022/American-Jewish-Millennials.

15 Vibe Israel and Hauswirth/Co, "Digital Campus Campaigns: Molding Young Minds About Israel," slide presentation, April 12, 2022, https://docs.google.com/presentation/d/1kUyRb gX9QdfcFEFvanS6JaSs4fTxwpNcyjrZnI9qudA/edit#slide=id.geb376ee94e_1_385.

CHAPTER 1

1 Equalman, "Is Social Media a Fad?," video, May 26, 2011, https://www.youtube.com/watch?v=CpVaBtDGvdc.

2 Aseel Bashraheel, "People Are Scrolling through 90 Meters Web Content Every Day – That's the Same as the Height of the Statue of Liberty," Arab News, April 11, 2018, https://www.arabnews.com/node/1283051/media.

3 National Merchants Association, "Gen Z Purchases Largely Influenced by Social Media," accessed September 28, 2022, https://www.nationalmerchants.com/gen-z-purchases-largely-influenced-social-media/.

4 Rishika Dugyala and Kamran Rahman, "6 Things to Know About Gen Z, Politics and 2020," *Politico*, October 11, 2020, https://www.politico.com/news/2020/10/11/gen-z-politics-2020-poll-takeaways-426767.

5   Yubo Team, "A Guide to Gen Z and Relationships," Yubo, accessed September 28, 2022, https://www.yubo.live/blog/a-guide-to-gen-z-and-relationships.

6   Emma Woodley, "91% of Surveyed College Students Use Dating Apps for More Than Just Hookups," Global Dating Insights, April 10, 2017, https://www.globaldatinginsights.com/news/91-of-surveyed-college-students-use-dating-apps-for-more-than-just-hookups/.

7   Ryan Jenkins, "This Is the Most Important Thing When Recruiting Generation Z," Inc.com, January 16, 2019, https://www.inc.com/ryan-jenkins/this-is-most-important-thing-when-recruiting-generation-z.html.

8   Dale Carnegie & Associates with Brent Cole, *How to Win Friends and Influence People in the Digital Age* (New York: Simon and Schuster, 2011), xii.

CHAPTER 2

1   Israel Ministry of Strategic Affairs and Public Diplomacy, *Behind the Mask: The Anti-Semitic Nature of the BDS Exposed*, September 2019, https://isgap.org/wp-content/uploads/2019/09/BDS-Antisemitism-Report-final-15.9.pdf.

2   Sam Sokol, "Aharoni: Israel Must Untangle Its Narrative from That of the Palestinians," *Jerusalem Post*, August 6, 2015, https://www.jpost.com/israel-news/politics-and-diplomacy/aharoni-israel-must-untangle-its-narrative-of-that-of-the-palestinians-411285.

3   For a short history of the iconic Blue Box, see: https://kkl-jnf.org/about-kkl-jnf/the-blue-box/.

4   Daniel Kahneman, *Thinking, Fast and Slow* (New York: Farrar, Straus and Giroux, 2013).

5   See e-estonia.com.

6 "Global Soft Power Index," Brand Finance, https://brandirectory. com/softpower/.

7 "Welcome to the GREAT Britain and Northern Ireland Campaign," GREAT Britain and Northern Ireland, https://www. greatcampaign.com/.

8 To name but a few: New Zealand Story, Essential Costa Rica, Brand South Africa, the UAE Nation Brand Office, the Swedish Institute, Promote Iceland, ThisisFINLAND, and Marca Chile.

9 For example, see the digital tool kits for these countries: New Zealand, Sweden, Estonia, Finland, Australia, Chile, and Israel (the latter created by Vibe Israel).

10 Such as Israel's decision in the early 1990s to encourage venture capital investment and create an innovation-based economy. And keep your eye on Saudi Arabia, with its Vision 2030 (declaring its shift to alternative energy exclusively by that date), as it successfully rebrands itself to the world (which requires it to engage not just in place-branding, but in major place-making as well, bringing the Saudi Kingdom well into the 21st century).

11 Such as GlobalScot for Scotland, and British businesses that are official partners of the GREAT Campaign.

12 Take a look at New Zealand's Fernmark License Program.

CHAPTER 3

1 Elias St. Elmo Lewis, *Financial Advertising* (Indianapolis: Levey & Bros., 1908), 95.

2 Tina Rosenberg, "Editorial Observer; Colombia's Tragedy, Captured in Close-Ups," *New York Times*, September 26, 1999, https://www.nytimes.com/1999/09/26/opinion/editorial-observer-colombia-s-tragedy-captured-in-close-ups.html.

3   See https://www.youtube.com/
    results?search_query=colombia+tourism+board.

4   Tariro Mzezewa, "How to Rebrand a Country," *New
    York Times,* November 23, 2019, https://www.nytimes.
    com/2019/11/23/travel/rebrandng-croatia-colombia.
    html?referringSource=articleShare.

5   José Filipe Torres, CEO of Bloom Consulting, emphasized this
    point to Israel stakeholders based on the consulting services his
    company has provided to Vibe Israel going back to 2018. See Ido
    Aharoni, "What 9/11 Taught Us about the Emotional Connection
    to Israel – Comment," *Jerusalem Post*, September 11, 2022,
    https://www.jpost.com/opinion/article-716918.

6   Rina Castelnuovo, "The Capital of Mediterranean Cool,"
    New York Times, July 20, 2008, https://www.nytimes.com/
    slideshow/2008/07/20/travel/0720-TELAVIV_index/s/0720-
    TELAVIV_slide1.html.

CHAPTER 4

1   Peter Laughter, "Radical Empathy," TedxFultonStreet, November
    11, 2015, https://www.youtube.com/watch?v=qkEG4sw5qn0.

2   Jacqui Paterson, "Radical Empathy: What Is It and What
    Are the Benefits?," Happiness.com, accessed October 17,
    2022, https://www.happiness.com/magazine/relationships/
    radical-empathy-extreme-what-is-it/.

3   "Next Gen," Goldman Sachs, accessed October 17, 2022, https://
    resources.goldman.com/nextgen.html.

4   Deloitte Insights, *Millennials and Beyond: Brand Growth through a
    Cross-Generational Approach to Consumer Profiling*, 2018, https://
    www2.deloitte.com/content/dam/insights/us/articles/4511_
    Millenials-and-beyond/DI_Millennials-and-beyond.pdf.

5   Paul Talbot, "Best Practices for Marketing to Gen-Z," *Forbes*, March 23, 2021, https://www.forbes.com/sites/paultalbot/2021/03/23/best-practices-for-marketing-to-gen-z/?sh=3f9c72c74319.

6   "What Workforce Diversity Means for Gen Z," Monster, accessed October 17, 2022, https://hiring.monster.com/resources/workforce-management/diversity-in-the-workplace/workforce-diversity-for-millennials/.

7   Patrick Thibodeau, "Cognitive Diversity," TechTarget, updated March 2018, https://www.techtarget.com/searchhrsoftware/definition/cognitive-diversity.

8   Alec Tyson, Brian Kennedy, and Cary Funk, "Gen Z, Millennials Stand Out for Climate Change Activism, Social Media Engagement With Issue," Pew Research Center, May 26, 2021, https://www.pewresearch.org/science/2021/05/26/gen-z-millennials-stand-out-for-climate-change-activism-social-media-engagement-with-issue/.

9   "Millennials Are Less Religious than Older Americans, but Just as Spiritual," Pew Research Center, November 23, 2015, https://www.pewresearch.org/fact-tank/2015/11/23/millennials-are-less-religious-than-older-americans-but-just-as-spiritual/.

10 "A Portrait of Jewish Americans," Pew Research Center, October 1, 2013, https://www.pewresearch.org/religion/2013/10/01/jewish-american-beliefs-attitudes-culture-survey/.

CHAPTER 5

[1] "Steve Jobs' Marketing Philosophy that Works!," YouTube video, https://www.youtube.com/watch?v=kshIWIc15yg.

[2] A review by Gallup of support patterns in the United States toward Israel in the past twenty years indicates that the sum of those who view Israel favorably and those who do not favor either side, ranged from 84% to 75% between 2001 and 2021, fluctuating over the years. A YouGov report on opinions of 18- to 24-year-old British people between 2019 and 2022 about Israel shows that 59% are indifferent toward the issue and 6% are positive, bringing the total to 64% neutral and positive.

[3] Mastercard, *Mastercard Index of Women Entrepreneurs 2020*, March 2021, https://www.mastercard.com/news/media/1ulpy5at/ma_miwe-report-2020.pdf.

[4] "Halo Effect," *Psychology Today*, accessed October 10, 2022, https://www.psychologytoday.com/us/basics/halo-effect.

[5] Vibe Israel, "Vibe Israel's Annual Perception Survey: Israeli Innovation Is the 'Iron Dome' of Israel's Image," Jewish News Syndicate, February 1, 2022, https://www.jns.org/wire/vibe-israels-annual-perception-survey-israeli-innovation-is-the-iron-dome-of-israels-image/.

CHAPTER 6

[1] i24 News English, "Inside the Instagram-Based Holocaust Diary Series 'Eva Stories,'" May 1, 2019, https://youtu.be/Pm3GjVHf4M0.

[2] "The Science of Stories: How Stories Impact Our Brains," Quantified, April 2, 2018, https://www.quantified.ai/blog/the-science-of-stories-how-stories-impact-our-brains/.

3   Celinne Da Costa, "3 Reasons Why Storytelling Is the Future of Marketing," *Forbes*, January 31, 2019, https://www.forbes.com/sites/celinnedacosta/2019/01/31/3-reasons-why-brand-storytelling-is-the-future-of-marketing/?sh=15d9d0055ffd.

4   Unfortunately, the hard copies went out of print and there is no digital version of the book for public consumption (that we are aware of).

5   For an executive summary of the research and main findings and recommendations by Bloom Consulting, go to: https://www.vibeisrael.com/wp-content/uploads/General-Research-Israel-Brand-2018.pdf.

6   Greer Fay Cashman, "Changing Perceptions by Branding Israel," *Jerusalem Post*, February 25, 2019, https://www.jpost.com/Israel-News/Changing-perceptions-by-branding-Israel-581272; "Vibe Israel Discloses Top Four Perceptions of Israel," *Jerusalem Post*, February 21, 2019, https://www.jpost.com//Israel-News/How-Millennials-view-Israel-havent-heard-of-BDS-study-finds-581239; and Jenni Frazer, "Jewish News Meets Joanna Landau: Woman on a Mission to Show Israel to the World!," *Jewish News*, March 15, 2019, https://www.jewishnews.co.uk/jewish-news-meets-joanna-landau-woman-on-a-mission-to-show-israel-to-the-world/.

7   "The 'Hamsa Aleinu' Airport Exhibit," Vibe Israel, 2021, https://www.vibeisrael.com/we_do/hamsa-aleinu-airport-exhibit/.

8   "Our Toolbox Has Everything You Need to Become an Israel Storyteller," Unboxing by Vibe Israel, accessed October 29, 2022, https://www.unboxing-israel.com/.

9   Katherine Hobson, "Clicking: How Our Brains Are in Sync," *Princeton Alumni Weekly*, April 11, 2018, https://paw.princeton.edu/article/clicking-how-our-brains-are-sync.

10 Uri Hasson, "Defend Your Research: I Can Make Your Brain Look Like Mine," *Harvard Business Review* 88 (2010): 32–33.

11 Tali Sharot, *The Influential Mind: What the Brain Reveals About Our Power to Change Others* (Henry Holt and Co., Kindle Edition, 2017): 42.

12 Jennifer Aaker, "Harnessing the Power of Stories," Michelle R. Clayman Institute for Gender Research, Stanford University, video, November 18, 2019, https://www.youtube.com/watch?v=oB7FfKPMZvw.

CHAPTER 7

1 Impressions are the number of times people saw the content. Organic impressions are those gained without paying for the content to appear, or for the influencer to share it.

2 Engagement level is measured by taking the number of people who responded to the posts they saw by liking, commenting, or sharing them, and dividing that number by the total number of people who saw the content.

3 Potential reach is the total number of followers or friends a user has on social media. Potential reach of a campaign is the total number of followers or friends that all the users who saw the campaign have.

4 "9 Weird and Wonderful Place Marketing Campaigns," City Nation Place, July 15, 2019, https://www.citynationplace.com/9-weird-and-wonderful-place-marketing-campaigns.

5 Kathi Kruse, "Rule of 7: How Social Media Crushes Old School Marketing," Kruse Control, September 29, 2021, https://www.krusecontrolinc.com/rule-of-7-how-social-media-crushes-old-school-marketing-2021/#:~:text=The%20Rule%20of%207%20states,movie%20industry%20in%20the%201930s.

6 Facebook and Google know this is annoying to their users, and they even allow you to indicate that you no longer want to see the ads, asking you why in order to tune their algorithm even better.

7   "What's the Difference between Organic, Paid and Post Reach?,"
     Facebook Help, accessed October 19, 2022, https://www.
     facebook.com/help/285625061456389.

8   Vindu Goel, "Facebook Will Curtail Unpaid Ads by Brands,"
     New York Times, November 14, 2014, https://www.nytimes.
     com/2014/11/15/technology/facebook-to-cut-unpaid-posts-by-
     marketers-on-news-feeds.html.

9   "Facebook Reach in 2022: How Many People See Your Posts?,"
     K6 Agency, accessed October 19, 2022, https://www.k6agency.
     com/facebook-reach/.

10 The Feed is what you see when you log in and start scrolling.

11 On the ministry's official website, if you scroll to the bottom, you
     will find links to its owned social platforms: https://www.gov.il/
     en/departments/ministry_of_foreign_affairs/govil-landing-page.
     It manages many others as well, in a more clandestine manner.

12 Go to this website for links to its social platforms: https://
     goisrael.com/.

CHAPTER 8

1   Tali Sharot, *The Influential Mind: What the Brain Reveals About
     Our Power to Change Others* (Henry Holt and Co., Kindle Edition,
     2017): 32.

2   Diane Musho Hamilton, "Calming Your Brain During Conflict,"
     Harvard Business Review, December 22, 2015, https://hbr.
     org/2015/12/calming-your-brain-during-conflict.

3   Corrie Brundage, "This Is What Happens in Your
     Brain When You Disagree," The Best Brain Possible,
     April 8, 2018, https://thebestbrainpossible.com/
     brain-disagree-politics-stress-empathy/.

4   *The Telegraph*, "Tel Aviv: Iron Dome Filmed Intercepting Barrage of Rockets over Israel," video, May 12, 2021, https://www.youtube.com/watch?v=B6wsujROvXg.

5   Tyler Manoukian, "Don't Criticize, Condemn, or Complain," Dale Carnegie Training Boston, April 2, 2012, https://dalecarnegieboston.tumblr.com/post/20350676146/dont-criticize-condemn-or-complain.

6   Vibe Israel, "Influence without Authority: How to Win Friends and Influence People About Israel," video series, last updated February 7, 2022, https://www.youtube.com/playlist?list=PLya95tUDJmD5Ez6aw2qDWzgZTOj3BswAp; and Vibe Israel, "Identity Resilience: How to Talk to Your Kids About Israel," video series, last updated February 7, 2022, https://www.youtube.com/playlist?list=PLya95tUDJmD4Q4mIYJcu4xOLcVCPx4WVN.

7   "Gal Gadot, Instagram Followers," Trackalytics, accessed October 20, 2022, https://www.trackalytics.com/instagram/profile/gal_gadot/.

CHAPTER 9

1   Ido Aharoni, "What 9/11 Taught Us about the Emotional Connection to Israel – Comment," *Jerusalem Post*, September 11, 2022, https://www.jpost.com/opinion/article-716918.

2   "Market Research Industry — Statistics and Facts," Statista, July 5, 2022, https://www.statista.com/topics/1293/market-research/.

3   Brand USA is an organization dedicated to marketing the United States as a premier travel destination. It is governed by an eleven-member board of directors, appointed by the US secretary of commerce: https://www.thebrandusa.com/about.

4   "Interactive Market Data," Brand USA, accessed October 22, 2022, https://www.thebrandusa.com/interactive-market-data.

5   New Zealand Story, "Research," accessed October 22, 2022, https://toolkit.nzstory.govt.nz/assets?tags=Research.

6   "Global Research: What Does the Next Generation Really Think of Israel?," Vibe Israel, accessed October 22, 2022, https://www.vibeisrael.com/we_do/research-on-global-perceptions-of-israel/.

7   Malcolm Gladwell, *The Tipping Point: How Little Things Can Make a Big Difference* (New York: Little, Brown and Company, 2000).

8   Gladwell, 92.

9   Gladwell, 89–132.

10   Ben Sales, "The Stats of US Anti-Semitism: A New Survey Has Some Clear and Dismal Data," *Times of Israel*, April 23, 2021, https://www.timesofisrael.com/the-stats-of-us-anti-semitism-a-new-survey-has-some-clear-and-dismal-data/.

11   *Digital Campus Campaigns: Molding Young Minds About Israel,* Vibe Israel and Hauswirth/Co, April 2022, https://www.vibeisrael.com/wp-content/uploads/H_Co-Vibe-Results_CLIENT-SHARE.pdf.

12   *Digital Campus Campaigns*, Vibe Israel and Hauswirth/Co.

CONCLUSION

1   American Jewish Congress, "AJC's Survey of American Jewish Millennials," 2022, https://www.ajc.org/Jewish-Millennial-Survey-2022/American-Jewish-Millennials.

2   "Our Toolbox Has Everything You Need to Become an Israel Storyteller," Unboxing by Vibe Israel, accessed October 29, 2022, https://www.unboxing-israel.com/.

3   Vibe Israel, "Influence without Authority: How to Win Friends and Influence People About Israel," video series, last updated February 7, 2022, https://www.youtube.com/playlist?list=PLya95tUDJmD5Ez6aw2qDWzgZTOj3BswAp.

Index

Symbols

A

B

Made in the USA
Middletown, DE
10 March 2023

26449825R00137